KALEIDOSCOPE

New Quilts from an Old Favorite

edited by

Barbara Smith and Ruth Ann Combs

American Quilter's Society

P. O. Box 3290 • Paducah, KY 42002-3290

Located in Paducah, Kentucky, the American Quilter's Society (AQS) is dedicated to promoting the accomplishments of today's quilters. Through its publications and events, AQS strives to honor today's quiltmakers and their work and to inspire future creativity and innovation in quiltmaking.

EDITORS: BARBARA SMITH AND RUTH ANN COMBS
BOOK DESIGN/ILLUSTRATIONS: CASSIE ENGLISH
COVER DESIGN: MICHAEL BUCKINGHAM
PHOTOGRAPHY: CHARLES R. LYNCH

Library of Congress Cataloging-in-Publication Data

Kaleidoscope: new quilts from an old favorite / edited by Barbara Smith and Ruth Ann Combs

p.cm.

ISBN 1-57432-727-5

1. Kaleidoscope quilts--Exhibitions. 2. Quilts--History--20th century-- Exhibitions. I. Smith, Barbara, 1941-   . II. Combs, Ruth Ann. III. American Quilter's Society. IV. Series.

NK9110.K36   1999

746.46'079'73--dc21   99-13893

CIP

Additional copies of this book may be ordered from the American Quilter's Society, PO Box 3290, Paducah, KY 42002-3290 @ $16.95. Add $2.00 for postage and handling.

Printed in the U.S.A. by Image Graphics, Paducah, KY

DEDICATION

This book is dedicated to quiltmakers
of all times and all places, whose works
continue to inspire and delight.

CONTENTS

PREFACE

This book was developed in conjunction with the annual Museum of the American Quilter's Society (MAQS) contest and exhibit called "New Quilts from Old Favorites." Dedicated to honoring today's quilters, MAQS created this contest to recognize, and share with others, the many fascinating interpretations that can grow out of a single traditional quilt block.

A brief description of the contest is followed by a presentation of the 18 finalists and their quilts, including the five award winners. Full-color photographs of the quilts accompany the quiltmakers' comments, which provide fascinating insights into the creative process. Full-size templates for the traditional Kaleidoscope block, and tips, techniques, and patterns contributed by the contest winners are provided so that you, too, will be able to enjoy making your own Kaleidoscope quilt.

It is our hope that this combination of outstanding quilts, full-size patterns, and instructions will inspire as many exciting quilts as the original contest did, adding new contributions to this pattern's continuing tradition.

For information about entering the current year's contest, write to MAQS, PO Box 1540, Paducah, KY 42002-1540.

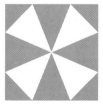

A special thanks goes to the corporations whose generous support has made this contest, exhibit, and book possible:

THE CONTEST

Each year, the "New Quilts from Old Favorites" contest challenges quilt-makers to develop innovative quilts from a different traditional pattern. The theme for 1999 was the Kaleidoscope block.

The only design requirement for quilts entered in the contest was that the quilt be recognizable in some way as being related to the Kaleidoscope. The quilt also had to be a minimum of 50" in each dimension and not exceed 100" in any one dimension, and it had to be quilted. A quilt could only be entered by the person who made it, and it had to have been completed after December 31, 1993. Many exciting interpretations of the pattern were submitted by quilters from around the world. From these entries, 18 quilts were selected; they are featured in this publication and also in a traveling exhibition.

For all who have experienced the thrill of peering into a kaleidoscope, the very mention of the word brings to mind spectacular images of color and light, colliding, blending, separating to form brilliant images of pure magic.

As with most things of beauty, the images of the kaleidoscope cannot be thoroughly and adequately defined with mere words. Even words like color, reflection, symmetry, pattern, and beauty fall short in their combined efforts to define the kaleidoscope and its imagery. With that in mind, is it any wonder that, for well over a century, quiltmakers have used fabric to re-create and define these mesmerizing designs?

Just as the possibilities for the images one might find in a kaleidoscope are endless, so too are the possibilities for quilt designs using the Kaleidoscope pattern. Those who are just being introduced to this geometric pattern may be surprised to learn that these dazzling displays of color are traditionally pieced using only two templates. As with the instrument itself, Kaleidoscope quilts employ color, reflection, and symmetry to create magical results from basic tools and skills.

The finalists in this year's contest demonstrate the range of possibilities offered by this traditional, versatile, and ever-changing quilt pattern.

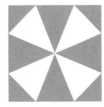

Barbara Oliver Hartman
Flower Mound, Texas
KALEIDOSTAR

Izumi Takamori
Tokyo, Japan
GEM STONES

Sachiko Suzuki
Chiba, Japan
A LOOK THROUGH A KALEIDOSCOPE

Anja Townrow
Walsall, United Kingdom
SPINNING WHEEL

Laura Park
Palm Harbor, Florida
SMOKE AND MIRRORS II

Finalists

Marta Amundson

Arleen Boyd

Sherry Chan

Ann Harwell

Virginia Holloway

Yoshiko Kobayashi

Susan Mathews

Lori S. Moum

Claudia Clark Myers

Laurie Sheeley

Judy Sogn

Beth Stewart-Ozark

Sue Turnquist

First Place 1

Kaleidostar
71" x 71", 1998
Cotton fabric and batting
Machine pieced and quilted

Barbara Oliver Hartman

Flower Mound, Texas

MY QUILTING

I began making quilts in about 1980 as a hobby. My grandmother made quilts, and I was always fascinated by her work. Soon after I starting quilting, my hobby became an obsession, and by 1989, I had retired from selling real estate to devote as much time as possible to quiltmaking. That same year, I started a small pattern company that is still active.

During the early 1980s, I met other quilters through the Quilter's Guild of Dallas and a local quilt shop. The friendships I have made through quiltmaking are the most precious of gifts.

I am also blessed with a wonderful and supportive family, whose pride in my work always shows. My husband, Bob; sister, Beverly; children; and grandchildren always enjoy my work, love to see me happy, and celebrate with me when good things happen. But there is no one like a mom for a cheerleader. My mother, Frances Oliver, saves every article written about me, cheers every award I earn, and is the best supporter anyone could ask for.

It is hard to believe that almost 20 years have flown by since I made my first quilt. I never envisioned at that time that my life would become so filled with such an interest.

Except for time spent with my family, most of my time is devoted to quilt-related activities. I usually have three or four quilt projects under way at any one time.

MY KALEIDOSCOPE QUILT

When I started my quilt in the summer of 1998, I had made only a few decisions about its design. I wanted it to look as though you were looking through a kaleidoscope, and I had chosen a particular fabric to use throughout the design and as a background. I also knew that the quilt would be foundation pieced, which has been my construction method of choice for the past three or four years.

To make this quilt, I drew a full-sized pattern with 16 sections. With the idea that I would use a foundation-piecing method, a design was drawn on one section and then mirrored on the section next to it. The mirrored sections were sewn together, creating eight larger units. The larger units were then sewn together in pairs, creating four quarters. At this point, to keep the center from being so bulky with seams, the tip of each quarter was cut away and replaced with a wedge of the background fabric so that the center would be smooth and flat.

I am very pleased with the way KALEIDOSTAR looked when completed. I have used variations of this format a few times in the past year and am finding many different ways to produce a circular image. It is always interesting to me how various combinations of fabrics and colors can change the overall result of a project. I plan to explore this type of design further.

"By using cheerful colors, the project was uplifting at a stressful time."

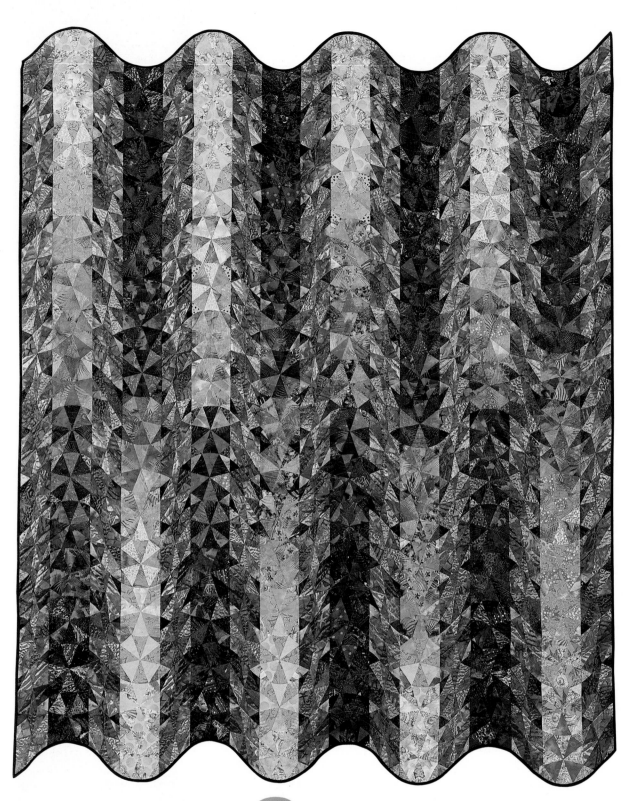

Second Place 2

Gem Stones
77½" x 92½", 1998
Cotton, acetate, rayon, and obi silk fabric
Machine pieced and quilted

Izumi Takamori

Tokyo, Japan

MY QUILTING

For several years, I had experimented with knitting, embroidery, sewing, and many other kinds of needle work. Then about 20 years ago, I saw for the first time an art quilt in a shop in Osaka, Japan. I was so moved by its beauty that I decided to take proper quilting classes.

I have been working with quilt designs on computer software, but I designed GEM STONES by hand and used a computer program to place the colors.

During the making of this quilt, I acquired a renewed appreciation for a bit of my own Japanese culture. I often use Japanese traditional obi silk in my quilts, but it was while working on GEM STONES that I realized how amazing the fabric really is.

I feel honored and proud to have been chosen as a finalist in this contest, just as I was in 1996 when my CRYSTAL STAR QUILT was awarded first place in the Ohio Star Quilt Competition at MAQS.

For my next project, I plan to try to use a computer program exclusively for the design process.

MY KALEIDOSCOPE QUILT

GEM STONES is made of cotton, acetate, rayon, and obi silk. I used foundation-paper piecing and a fast machine-piecing method to construct the top. Metallic thread accentuates the machine quilting.

The guild of which I am a member makes a challenge quilt each year. This year's challenge was to use 10 different fabrics chosen by the members. (Can you find the 10 different fabrics?) I decided on the Kaleidoscope pattern because of the MAQS contest.

I am pleased with the outcome of this quilt because of the way I altered the pattern and because of the flow of colors. If I were to use this design again, I would like to try making it off center.

"I really love the fact that I never know how my designs on paper are going to turn out in fabric."

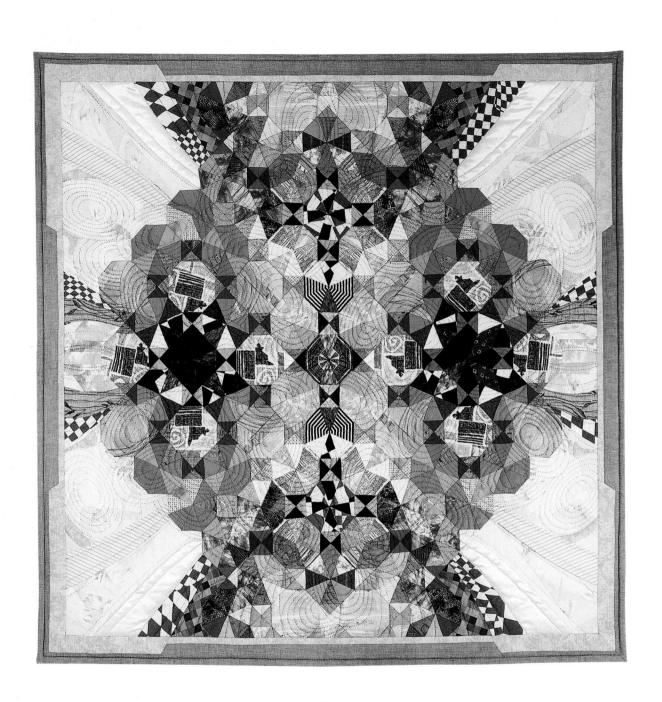

A Look Through A Kaleidoscope
55" x 55", 1998
Cotton and cotton blend fabric
Hand piecing, appliqué, and quilting

Sachiko Suzuki
Chiba, Japan

MY QUILTING

I have loved knitting since I was a small child when I would unravel old sweaters to add new yarns to create new patterns and play with colors.

In the late 1970s and early 1980s, my family lived in New Jersey where I first encountered quilts and joined classes at the YWCA. I discovered that making quilts has something in common with my knitting in that I could reuse old clothes and scraps to create new things.

While living in New Jersey, I visited Pennsylvania, much of New England, and some places in Canada, where I saw many antique quilts. After returning to Japan, I continued my study of quiltmaking. Then in 1988, I lived in San Jose, California, where we stayed for two years. I joined the Santa Clara Valley Quilt Association and a small quilters' group called Cover Girls. I also worked as a volunteer at the American Museum of Quilts and Textiles where I saw outstanding works and made many dear friends.

From my stay in New Jersey, I learned about traditional quilts. In California, I learned about art quilts. My quiltmaking reveals a blend of the two experiences.

I have written how-to articles about handicrafts, and in 1996, I published a book in Japan called *Patterns for Scraps*. It introduces 25 quilt patterns with instructions, tips on color choices, and quilting designs.

MY KALEIDOSCOPE QUILT

With A LOOK THROUGH A KALEIDOSCOPE, I pursued a new twist on the traditional Kaleidoscope design. I wanted to emphasize soft shades by using natural, light colors like sand beige, dull orange, and blue-gray. I added the checkerboard and stripes to accentuate the symmetrical design and to help create a cool, modern look. The 83 five-inch squares were hand pieced, creating a mosaic effect. Stuffed appliqué helps the design radiate from the center.

I always take particular care in the design and placement of my quilting lines. For this piece, I wanted to create a sense of movement, so I chose a design that features a series of five ovals echoing a small center oval. They were randomly placed on the quilt top. I used a gray thread for the hand quilting. The border combines two colors to help radiate the light and to allow the movement to appear to continue beyond the edges.

"During the four and one-half years I lived in New Jersey, I encountered quilts and became obsessed."

Fourth Place 4

Spinning Wheel
66" x 66", 1998
Cotton fabric and batting
Machine pieced, quilted, and
appliquéd

Anja Townrow
Walsall, United Kingdom

MY QUILTING

A native of Holland, I came to England when I was 21. Soon after, I married. I started to put scraps of old clothing together when pregnant with my first child. I made "patch-work bedspreads," for I had never heard of quilts. I explored squares and triangles and then progressed to drawing simple blocks on graph paper. Ten years ago, I joined the Quilter's Guild of the British Isles. At quilt shows, I found patterns, and back issues of American quilting magazines. I worked my way through those magazines, soaking up all that knowledge and putting it to use. I made quilts to give away, then to sell, and then to teach quiltmaking at a local community center. I also write for three quilting magazines.

American quilters continue to inspire me. When I saw the works of Caryl Bryer Fallert, Jane Sassaman, Faye Anderson, and Yvonne Porcella, to name a few, I knew those were the kinds of quilts I wanted to make: bold designs with bright colors.

My three daughters all show interest in art. The eldest studies art at Manchester Metropolitan University, and the two youngest, who are eight and six years old, draw pictures they call quilt designs. They have made foundation-pieced blocks for a quilt that we are working on.

My husband is an expert on anything to do with quiltmaking. He can spot a piece of Hoffman fabric from 10 paces, and he is my most outspoken critic.

MY KALEIDOSCOPE QUILT

I always make a full-sized master pattern on freezer paper. Elements that can be foundation pieced are sewn first, then treated as one piece to be joined to the rest of the design.

For SPINNING WHEEL, I taped sheets of graph paper together and designed the wedge with the aid of a protractor. I drew my design inside the wedge with compasses and a ruler, making sure the drawing was symmetrical. I made a trial block and saw that the design had serious problems. The second design had better proportions, and once I decided on the batik fabric for the background, I chose the other colors from my stash. There are actually 12 fabrics to be found in this quilt.

After assembling all the wedges, I was stuck on the border and corners. This happens a lot as I don't like to plan a quilt too far ahead. A hunt around fabric shops failed to produce what I was looking for. Eventually I settled for a blue batik that had been sitting on my shelves all along.

For quilting, I used invisible thread and various colors of metallic threads.

The quilt was named by my daughter Harriet. Usually, the name of a quilt suggests itself to me during the making, but this one was always "the Kaleidoscope quilt." After it was completed, I asked the family to come up with some names. I really pleased my little girl by picking her suggestion.

"I make quilts to satisfy a creative urge. For me, a day without quilting is an incomplete day."

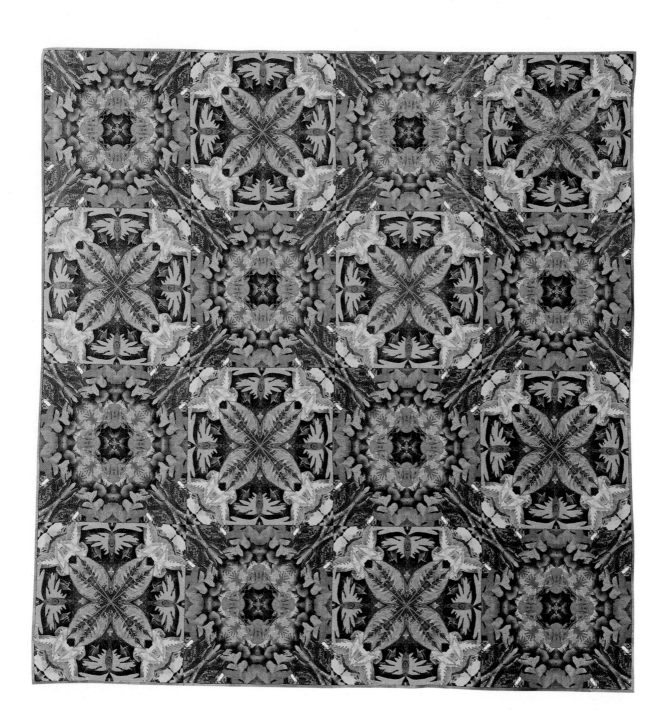

Fifth Place **5**

Smoke and Mirrors II
64" x 64", 1998
Cotton fabric, batting, and specialty
quilting threads
Machine pieced and quilted

Laura A. Park

Palm Harbor, Florida

MY QUILTING

SMOKE AND MIRRORS II is the fourth piece I have completed since I started quilting in 1996. I am a fourth generation seamstress, and I am fascinated with surface design and solving design problems.

While recovering from a life-threatening illness, I attended a meeting of the Fiber Arts Group at my church. There I met a dedicated quiltmaker, Rosella Inman, 80 years of age, who is now my mentor. She introduced me to Quilter's Crossing, a local club dedicated to excellence in design and workmanship.

Members share their expertise, and the club sponsors workshops with nationally known teachers. Classes with Paula Nadelstern and Caryl Bryer Fallert have had an enormous influence on my appreciation of design and symmetry. Michael James gave me new insight on color and was the catalyst in broadening my interest in hand dyeing fabric.

From a class on dyeing, printing, and painting fabrics, I gained a more professional approach to formulas, and I have been able to produce and repeat the colors that I want.

At a workshop, Caryl Bryer Fallert said that often she did not know what a quilt was about until it was finished. Her remark rang true as I finished my Kaleidoscope quilt and realized, for the first time, what my quilt was about. The color and complexity are reflections of my life.

MY KALEIDOSCOPE QUILT

Seeking to explore new areas of technology while adhering to a traditional block arrangement, I designed SMOKE AND MIRRORS II with computer design software. To counter any copyright conflict, I created my kaleidoscope designs from leaves and flowers instead of scanning fabrics into my computer.

My quilt was humbly born of plain, white fabric that allowed me limitless creativity. Limitless also are the design possibilities of computer software and the techniques of printing directly on fabric with a computer printer. With today's technology, one is bound only by one's reach and imagination.

The Kaleidoscope is unique, a one-of-a-kind block that cannot be easily duplicated. I designed 75 blocks, then selected two favorites, alternating them in a 16-block setting that produces a secondary butterfly design where four blocks merge.

The backing is made of asymmetrical blocks of hand-dyed fabrics. The quilt is free-motion machine quilted, using regular quilting thread, gold metallic thread, and rayon thread for embroidery. The quilting was done on a custom-modified machine altered to allow 20" from needle to column.

In retrospect, before attempting to use the computer program for quilt design, I would have looked for a computer class.

"As we approach the new millennium, I feel that quiltmakers are on the cutting edge of an exciting era of computer design."

Almost Paradise
63" x 63", 1998
Cotton fabric
Machine quilted, pieced,
and appliquéd

Marta Amundson

Riverton, Wyoming

MY QUILTING

My quilts reflect my passion for the environment and the animals that live in it. I am lucky to live in Wyoming where there are far more wild animals than people. I start every day with a walk to observe the changing wonder of nature. That walk assures the inspiration I need to spend all day in the studio, even if the task may be tedious.

Quiltmaking gives me freedom to travel and meet people. On a lecture tour in Australia last summer, I was delighted with the hospitality and taken in by the beauty of the landscape and animals. The experience became my inspiration for ALMOST PARADISE.

This year, I will teach quilting in Scotland, sail the Ganges, and look for tigers from the back of an elephant in Nepal. I give myself the opportunity to learn new things from my travels. The fascinating people who I visit share their ideas and teach me about their local flora and fauna. Later, what I learn becomes a part of my work. Like taking a photograph, quilting gives me a way to share with others.

Last year, I started writing a column for quilters' newsletters in London, Adelaide, Colorado, and Wyoming. At first I thought it would be hard to think of something new to say every month, but no, it is exactly like making a quilt. You just say what is in your heart.

MY KALEIDOSCOPE QUILT

As a silent observer for three weeks in Australia, I heard about environmental issues that made my hair stand on end. Although the people I visited were friendly and it was good fun to feed the kangaroos, watching television or listening to the radio was a painful experience.

Among my concerns: Many Australians see their current government as one that is anti-environment; a bill was passed that strips most indigenous people of their land rights; a new uranium mine is opening in Kakadu National Park.

I started my quilt with these observations and did my best to give them a voice.

The fabric I used is mostly Australian screen prints. I added American fabric when I could not get visual separation of the appliqué animals from the background, and used contrasting threads to give more definition. Because colors of the individual blocks were diverse, I used a hand-dyed sashing to bring them into harmony.

The five different animals were cut from freezer paper and ironed on fabric with a fusible web on the back. I positioned them on the blocks and ironed them down before machine appliquéing. I first ironed freezer paper on the back of the blocks to act as a stabilizer. I discarded the paper after doing my satin stitching.

"I look for beauty in things unconventional – finding a rhino as lovely as a lotus."

Finalist

Persian Fantasy II
57" x 68", 1996
Cotton fabric
Machine pieced
and hand quilted

Arleen Boyd

Rochester, New York

MY QUILTING

My grandmother, who lived with us until I was seven years old, tried to teach me to sew but ended up saying, "Arleen, you will never sew. You don't put knots in the thread." My mother encouraged sewing and embroidery, which she did very well. She made all of my clothes and many for my dolls. She died when I was 12, and since I was a naive girl, I assumed the only way to have clothes was to make them, so I began. Some projects were successful, but some went in the rag bag.

As a wife and mother, I sewed for our three girls and gradually started to teach sewing at home and in continuing-education classes. While visiting my husband's aunt, I saw her quilting in what I now know to be a quilt-as-you-go method, and the ease of a small unit appealed to me. I made my first quilt in that way and used kettle cloth for the backing. No wonder the quilting was slow going.

I needed some good instruction and in 1980 found that in Sonia Cimino. Quilting was a nice blend of several interests because it combined fabric, sewing, and design. I make quilts because there are ideas in my mind that have to be let out.

Taking classes from nationally known teachers has broadened my horizons. The works of Jinny Beyer and Paula Nadelstern have had an effect on my recent works. A quilt in progress has nine Kaleidoscopes, eight circling a larger center one.

MY KALEIDOSCOPE QUILT

The idea for this quilt came in the mail. We received an ad for Oriental carpets, and one picture particularly said "quilt" to me. I drew up a design as similar as possible on the computer. After a couple of modifications, I had a design I liked.

In order to have a more detailed diagram to work from, I drew a single segment of the Kaleidoscopic center with possible design elements. After duplicating several of them, I cut them out and pasted them on a scrap sheet. This gave me a way to try out the possible color combinations and view the total look.

I already had the wonderful patterned fabric with several symmetrical designs on my shelf and decided that it would be perfect for the very center of the medallion. With that as the basis, the other fabrics were chosen to blend with it. All fabrics are 100% cotton.

The quilting enhances the lines of the designs in the prints. In the places where there are narrow parallel lines, they are stuffed by running yarn through the channels.

If I were to use this design again, I would, of necessity, have to change the center. It would be impossible to find fabric to duplicate the design and shape of the pattern as it is. I would probably put different designs in the borders that create the rectangle, simply because I don't enjoy doing the same thing twice.

"Quilting is friendship, sharing, learning, teaching, and an opportunity to give to others – family, friends, and the community."

Finalist

Life's Little Surprises
62" x 65", 1998
Cotton fabric and wool batting
Machine pieced and quilted

Sherry Chan
San Francisco, California

MY QUILTING

It was the Kaleidoscope block that prompted my quilting adventures. After skimming through Paula Nadelstern's book *Kaleidoscope & Quilts*, I decided to learn to quilt. The Kaleidoscope quilts pictured in her book were absolutely beautiful. After reading it, I decided to take some quilting classes before tackling such a complex quilting project.

A few weeks later, I signed up for a couple of classes. I made a sampler and a trip-around-the-world quilt. After completing these, I was ready for the challenge of Kaleidoscope quilts, and, I thought that a Kaleidoscope quilt would make a nice Christmas gift for a friend.

Part of the fun in designing that first Kaleidoscope was in finding just the right fabrics. I must have gone to every fabric sale from Berkeley to San Diego, California. I find it important to visit different quilt shops because of the wide variety of fabrics that is available. Shops in conservative neighborhoods tend to carry traditional prints, whereas quilt shops in fun and funky neighborhoods tend to carry "far-out" prints more suitable for creating a Kaleidoscope quilt.

I am an environmental health scientist with the California Department of Health Services, where I write health assessment documents for hazardous waste sites.

In my spare time, I bake, quilt, travel, and have taken up upholstery.

MY KALEIDOSCOPE QUILT

An employee at my local quilt shop had read about the New Quilts from an Old Favorite: Kaleidoscope Quilts contest and, knowing of my interest in the Kaleidoscope block, suggested I enter the contest. LIFE'S LITTLE SURPRISES is the result of that suggestion.

From Paula Nadelstern's book, I learned I needed fabrics that featured repeating patterns and directional prints.

I used the same techniques that I used in the quilt I made for my friend. My contest quilt took me three months, approximately 150 hours, to complete. I decided to make it whimsical and fun.

"In each kaleidoscope, there is something special. Look a little closer and you will understand."

Finalist

**Balance the Scales
of World Justice**
62" x 62", 1998
Cotton fabric and batting
Machine pieced and hand quilted

28

Ann Harwell

Wendell, North Carolina

MY QUILTING

I began quilting in 1976 when expecting my first son. That first quilt was fun to make and so fulfilling. He loved it almost to smithereens!

My love of fabrics and sewing can be traced to my grandmother, who made quilts and taught me to hand sew and crochet. I made doll clothes and potholders with every scrap of fabric I was given. Grandmother once told me I could have all the scrap fabric I liked if I would walk down to the old homeplace and search through an old box. I was scared to go alone, but braved the adventure for the prize.

My mother used to tell me I bothered her continually as a pre-schooler when she was sewing. I remember sneaking into her room to try to play with her Featherweight Singer (I couldn't reach the pedal). I got my first sewing machine when I was eight, a hand-cranked beige Singer that still works.

Others who have influenced my quilting are church members who made quilts for my family when my dad and grandfather, who were ministers, would move to new church assignments; Janet Laing, a handbag designer; my mother-in-law, who taught me to hand quilt; my dad, whose sermons I listened to while gazing at stained glass windows; and my mother, who taught me the importance of ripping out offending seams and how to precision cut fabric, ever-mindful of the grain.

MY KALEIDOSCOPE QUILT

I wanted to symbolize justice, liberty, and equality, three of the ideas Mortimer Adler wrote about in his philosophical book *Six Great Ideas*. Justice is represented by scales; liberty by fabrics symbolizing expression such as music fabric, pen nibs with feathers, pencils, art, hiero-glyphs, and Miss Liberty; and equality by images of people, the globes, and the doves of peace. Words from Declaration of Independence fabric and from African-families fabric illustrate sections of the octagon.

My inspiration for this quilt came when my son was in the Persian Gulf, aboard the aircraft carrier *George Washington*. I was concerned about the United Nations' ability to bring about world justice. Adler's book had convinced me that liberty and equality are not possible without justice, and I wanted to make a quilt that illustrated that concept.

This quilt is a plea for world justice. Doves of peace hold the scales of justice, because, without them, peace is rendered an impossible goal. The same scale must weigh us all. Our children must be educated so that everyone may share the benefits of freedom and the ability to express this freedom.

"I make quilts simply because I am driven to do so for some unknown reason."

29

Opening
70" x 90", 1998
Cotton fabric and batting
Machine pieced and quilted

Virginia Holloway
Randolph, Massachusetts

MY QUILTING

I spent the first 20 years of my art career as a painter. It eventually became clear to me, however, that my style and method of painting required the use of unhealthy and unsafe materials. I abandoned the medium, continuing to do only small drawings, at most.

My mother and grandmothers made quilts and sewed, so I always had quilts around me while I was growing up. In 1985, when the efforts of my full-time job had just about stopped all my creative work, my drawings began to look like quilts. Somewhere along the line, I began to read about, study, and eventually make quilts, as a new attempt at creative expression.

I am drawn to quiltmaking because of its inherent incorporation of opposites: tradition and invention, function and decoration, discipline and freedom, complexity and simplicity. It is this juxtaposition of opposites that creates the tension in my work. It is this tension that spawns new ideas and motivates me to complete the arduous work of a large piece. There is a great deal of room to move in the gulf between extremes.

My current designs are simpler overall but have more complex and subtle color balances. I am hopeful to eventually do some fabric painting and dyeing to add yet another dimension to my creative expression.

MY KALEIDOSCOPE QUILT

I have always been fond of bright rainbow color combinations. When I saw the Rainbow Gardens floral Hoffman fabric, which I used in the border of OPENING, I bought 10 yards and have used bits of it in several projects. I never managed to use it to my satisfaction, though, until this quilt.

In 1994, to help me with my teaching skills, I took a class called Strip-Pieced Kaleidoscope. It turned out to be even more useful to me because I learned to work directly with fabric pieces on a design wall. Kaleidoscope is particularly suited to this design method. I make several wedge-shaped units from a group of selected colors and fabrics, then move them around on the wall until I like the effect.

I have made about 15 large Kaleidoscope quilts and many more small ones. One that was pieced for a guild raffle was accepted into an American Quilter's Society show.

Since the entire process of making this quilt was based on change and experimentation, I do not think I would want to change this piece at all. I will do more of them because I enjoyed making this design so much, and I will be in a different color-mood each time.

> "I am fascinated by old Amish quilts, and inspired to relearn old techniques and to explore new ones."

Early Spring Wood
59" x 59", 1998
Cotton fabric and polyester batting
Machine pieced and hand quilted

Yoshiko Kobayashi
Osaka, Japan

MY QUILTING

I started making quilts about 10 years ago after becoming inspired during a quilt exhibition in Nagoya, Japan. I studied quiltmaking for four years and continue the process of self-teaching as my work evolves and progresses.

I always loved to draw and enjoyed making various handicrafts during my school days. So it seems quite natural, I think, to make quilts today.

Until quite recently, all my quilts were hand pieced and hand quilted. After attending a workshop by Nancy Crow in Osaka, I have been trying some machine piecing, but continue to do hand quilting.

I enjoy making quilts with a particular theme in mind. I was drawn to participate in the Kaleidoscope Quilts contest because it allowed me to think freely within the loose confines set forth in the contest rules. I'm looking forward to more challenges.

MY KALEIDOSCOPE QUILT

This quilt was made especially for the MAQS contest. I had wanted to make a Kaleidoscope quilt, so the contest gave me the motivation I needed to get started.

When I began designing EARLY SPRING WOOD, the Nagano Winter Olympic Games were well under way. I thought of snow, cold wind, icy fields, and mountains, and that spring would come soon after.

I also recalled the lyrics of my favorite song "Early Spring Music," which says spring is here but the wind remains cold. The uguisu (Japanese bush warbler) imagines his songs but will not utter his notes because he thinks it is not time to sing.

I thought the Kaleidoscope block would be a suitable pattern to express my images of this song.

This quilt was made with paper-foundation piecing, my own machine-pieced fabrics, and commercial fabrics. My machine-pieced fabrics are made by using a technique learned from Nancy Crow. Various shapes of leaves are quilted to show trees waiting for spring in the wood.

"I am interested in making new quilts in traditional patterns. Although sometimes it can be difficult, I like the challenge."

Susan Mathews

Victoria, Australia

MY QUILTING

My love for quiltmaking evolved from an earlier love of weaving, which required too much equipment to be portable. As my brother's twenty-first birthday was approaching, I decided to make a quilt for the occasion. He was so pleased with my effort that he commissioned me to make a quilt for his girlfriend's twenty-first birthday. I have not stopped making quilts since then.

I enjoy playing with color and pattern, and my quilts are celebrations of that rather than the expression of any deep and meaningful ideas. My love of color and pattern has led me to develop my own hand-dyed and printed fabrics, and I mostly use these fabrics in my work.

As this book is being published, work progresses on a variation of the traditional Crown of Thorns pattern, made entirely from my hand-dyed fabrics. It evolves slowly on my design wall and is nothing like the sketch I started with. I am happy with its progress and am now toying with border and finishing ideas.

I'm also working to develop designs from irregular and frayed strips of fabric fused to a backing. I want to add more color and more design elements with heavy free-motion machine embroidery. These strips will form my "fabric," from which I will produce a quilt or, hopefully, a number of quilts.

MY KALEIDOSCOPE QUILT

MIDNIGHT FLOWERS is a reflection of my feelings during a time of great turmoil in my life. It was a means of working through some of the problems in a way. The quilt was put away for some time and finished some years later in much happier circumstances.

It was one of the first quilts in which I used a pieced back, something I often do now.

When designing Kaleidoscopes, I use a grid design technique I learned from an article by Robin Golobic Alcorn. The grid allows you to design illusory curves where none exist. I had previously made several quilts from a block designed by Jeffrey Gutcheon, called Judy in Arabia, which creates the same effect. I have also played around with the Pineapple block in the same way, and there are other blocks that have this potential.

A particular challenge I faced when making this quilt was trying to piece triangles into the border print fabric while maintaining the continuity of the pattern on the fabric. While wrestling with this, I took a seminar with Jinny Beyer and asked her advice. She said she probably would have appliquéd the triangles.

If I were to use this design again, I would use hand-dyed fabrics because these are the fabrics I am using now, and I like the subtle shadings and richness of color.

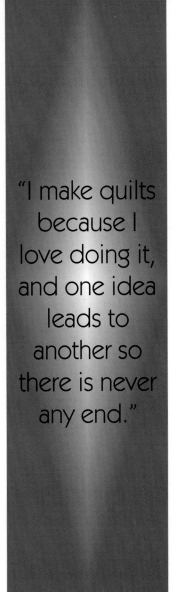

"I make quilts because I love doing it, and one idea leads to another so there is never any end."

Crystal Vision
74" x 74", 1998
Cotton fabric
Machine pieced and quilted

Lori S. Moum

Marysville, Washington

MY QUILTING

My first quilt was made on a whim in 1992. A fellow Navy wife and I decided to each make a bed quilt to pass the time while our husbands were deployed for two months. Mine was designed and the top was completed by the time my husband returned, but it took several months for completion. Little did I know what I had gotten myself into. I began making wearable art and marbling fabric in 1994, dyeing fabric in 1996, and teaching in 1997.

Those who have influenced my work include Caryl Bryer Fallert, Libby Lehman, Meryl Ann Butler, Michael James, and Nancy Crow. One of my goals is to study with these individuals, who are masters of their art, in my view.

I am working on the finishing touches of a four-foot-square tray for marbling silk. The fabric will be used in an original wearable, which I hope to have finished before the year 2000.

MY KALEIDOSCOPE QUILT

With my entry, I wanted to maintain the integrity and theme of the Kaleidoscope block while altering it just enough so that the viewer would see different images, depending on their focus. I also wanted to hide the block so that the viewer would have to work to find it.

Using aspects of a real kaleidoscope, such as reflection, multi-layers of contrast and transparency, and a three-dimensional effect, I turned to the computer to begin my design.

Once I had a design I liked, I worked on values by using only black and white. I moved to color placement only when I had achieved the depth I was looking for.

Color placement was also done on the computer, but not exclusively. I chose batik fabrics simply because I love them. The colors and texture have such a natural organic sense that appeals to me, and they capture the jewel-like bits of colored glass that can be seen in a kaleidoscope.

I collected as many different textures and values of batik fabrics in the colors that I like and made several full-size test blocks. Not only did this show me how the block really worked but how fabric textures and colors were going to be oriented so that the blocks would flow from one to another. Certain colors had to have specific placement in order for transparency and proper contrast to occur.

"The decision to use only batiks for this quilt resulted in quite a challenge for me."

The Gathering Storm

60" x 65", 1998
Cotton fabric and cotton blend batting
Machine pieced, appliquéd,
embroidered, quilted, and hand beaded

Claudia Clark Myers
Duluth, Minnesota

MY QUILTING

Convinced I would love it, a friend dragged me to the Minnesota Quilters show in 1991. Well, she was right. I had expected quilts like the pink and blue Sunbonnet Sue I had on my bed as a child. I was amazed at the artistic pieces that fell into the quilt category. I could see a relationship between the art quilts and my work as a professional costumer.

For more than 25 years, I had designed and constructed pieces for ballet, theater, and opera. Here were their relatives, up on the walls at a quilt show! As I retire from the performing arts, I find I have transferred many skills learned for the stage to my quilting. I am fortunate that I can continue to see my ideas come to life, still work with all that wonderful fabric and color, and there are no more dress rehearsal deadlines!

Often, when I begin a quilt, I pin clumps of fabric on the wall. I rearrange them many times before I decide what design I will make. As a result of taking many classes, I have begun to work in the curved-pieced and machine-appliquéd style of THE GATHERING STORM. This has been a wonderfully freeing experience for me because anything I can draw, I can make into a quilt. However, I'm not sure the day will ever come when I will be comfortable not turning my edges under. The "make it to last through 50 performances" ethic is still too strong.

MY KALEIDOSCOPE QUILT

"Kaleidoscope" could be interpreted so many ways, I thought as I contemplated this design. I kept seeing propellers – helicopter propellers, ship propellers, even beanie hats with propellers. None of these seemed appropriate for a quilt.

There is a wind farm near my home with huge machines on a hill, making electricity. They remind me of their origins, Dutch windmills. From that thought, the quilt just seemed to fall together: windmills, tulips, and Delft tiles, all kaleidoscopes.

I did my sketches, made transparencies and projected them onto large sheets of paper, which I used as patterns. I projected and pieced the windmills separately and then appliquéd them onto the background, embroidering all their details, either freehand or stitching over tracing paper. I pieced the tulips, faced them with green fabric, and stitched them on top of the quilt to give them a three-dimensional appearance. I used templates for the Delft tile blocks. I did this quilt entirely by machine. In my world, handwork is only for beads, bindings, and labels.

"I wanted to piece the background with rectangular Kaleidoscope blocks, but that would have taken me until 2003."

Finalist

Summer Vacation
62" x 72", 1998
Cotton fabric and batting, rayon
and metallic thread
Machine pieced and quilted

40

Laurie Sheeley

Parkman, Wyoming

MY QUILTING

I have been obsessed with quilt-making since the day I took my first stitch. My mother got me hooked. She would bring her quilts to show when she came from Alaska to visit. I was working and raising children, and I never considered making quilts. But I would look at her quilts in absolute awe. I remember a Triple Rail Fence with a white-on-white muslin in it. I had never seen anything so beautiful.

One day in 1987, I purchased a pattern and materials for a full-sized bed quilt. That night, I started on one of the greatest adventures of my life.

At first, my mother was the only other quiltmaker I knew, and I would consult long distance on techniques and color choices. Then in 1990, I got together with another obsessed quiltmaker, Mary Jane Collins. If you do not have a quilting best friend, get one. Sharing is a wonderful part of quilting.

My husband and children are my advisors and sources of encouragement. My husband, Bruce, a rather oversized, outdoorsy cowboy, has become rather artistic and can talk the technical language of quiltmaking and color with anyone. My sisters are my fan club and are always on the lookout for unusual fabrics.

I have started to sell quilts to help support my habit. I also teach classes on watercolor quilts and machine quilting.

MY KALEIDOSCOPE QUILT

This quilt got its name because I finished it on a special summer vacation when I went to my in-laws' cabin in the Big Horn Mountains – alone. The cabin is used as a cow camp, and the many times I was there feeding cowboys, I would dream of packing up food, water, and quilting supplies and staying until I ran out of any of the above.

All of the quilting was done there, which makes that part of the quilt very special to me. I broke about 10 sewing machine needles in the process and was down to one needle and completely out of water when I finished the quilt.

Putting the colors together was interesting and fun. Color and value were very important. Originally, I thought I would have the yellow in the center surrounded by orange, then red, violet, blue, and green. It soon became evident that this would yield a quilt the size of Texas, so I adjusted the color placement to create a sort of rainbow effect.

To check for color and value placement, I looked through a small pair of binoculars turned backward. I switched and turned the completed blocks, and looked through the binoculars until I was nearly crazy. At that point, I stitched it together and put it in the closet where it spent quantity time with other unfinished projects until I took that special summer vacation.

> "When I worked, I quilted late at night and Sundays. Now that I have no outside job, I quilt late at night and on Sundays."

Finalist

Kaleidoscopes, Diamonds & Stars
51" x 59", 1998
Cotton fabric and polyester batting
Machine pieced and hand quilted

Judy Sogn
Seattle, Washington

MY QUILTING

I have always been interested in hand work. My aunt taught me to embroider when I was very young. I taught myself to knit from a book when I was in junior high, and I started sewing clothing after seventh grade home economics. I made most of my own clothes for many years. I also enjoyed needlepoint for several years, until I had no room left for another pillow or picture.

Quiltmaking caught my interest in 1982 when I was looking for something unusual to make for family and friends. I especially enjoy the creativity possible with quilting, and I like not being dependent upon another artist's expensive painted canvas for my designs.

One quilting technique led to another. Today, I no longer make clothing except for an occasional quilted vest. Knitting and needlepoint have also been left behind.

I make quilts because I love the entire process from research, to planning, to executing every stage of a quilt's development. One of my favorite steps is the removal of the basting threads. It seems like such a little thing, but I am always amazed to see the transformation that happens when the last basting thread is removed and the finished quilt emerges.

MY KALEIDOSCOPE QUILT

KALEIDOSCOPES, DIAMONDS & STARS was made especially for the MAQS contest. I used computer-design software, which allowed me to quickly and easily see the block as a diamond rather than the conventional square format. The diamond unit hides the block so well that I sometimes have trouble finding the Kaleidoscope unit.

I am especially fond of multi-fabric quilts, so I chose as many different fabrics as I could find for each of the six color areas in the quilt. I chose fabrics that are only subtly different within each color family because I did not want a spotty look to the quilt. I wanted the viewer to be surprised to find dozens of fabrics on close inspection, rather than only the six that are apparent from a distance.

The first things that caught my eye during the design process were the stars that form when the diamonds meet in the corners. From there I looked for larger areas that could be defined and would be unusual, breaking away from individual unit colorations.

Finally, I looked for an outline that would be pleasing yet different from the standard square or rectangular quilt shape. I found several shapes that were interesting, and the hardest part was deciding which one to make.

"Making and attaching the binding is a step I thoroughly enjoy, perhaps because the finished product is close at hand."

Busby Berkeley's Butterfly Ballet
74" x 74", 1998
Cotton and tulle fabric; cotton, metallic,
and chenille thread
Machine pieced, quilted, and appliquéd

Beth Stewart-Ozark

Lexington, South Carolina

MY QUILTING

A friend shared her love of quilt-making with me in 1991. In one afternoon of hand piecing and hand quilting, I knew I had found a passion that would not desert me. When my husband, Norm, and I moved to South Carolina from California in 1995, I had collected 30 boxes of quilting paraphernalia.

In South Carolina, I joined my first guild, Logan Lap Quilters. There my creativity blossomed. Gradually, I began to teach myself to machine quilt and to use different techniques.

I am what I call an eclectic quilter, meaning that I enjoy both the traditional and the contemporary aspects of creating quilts. Whatever the design of the quilt, I seem led by some hand not quite my own.

A fellow quiltmaker invited me to the 1997 AQS show in Paducah. What a feast! Taking classes and attending lectures from people I had only met in books, visiting MAQS and seeing an incredible array of expert workmanship gave me encouragement to explore.

I still have an enormous amount to learn, and I am grateful to Charlotte Warr Andersen, Libby Lehman, Judy B. Dales, Moneca Calvert, Ruth McDowell, Mary Ellen Hopkins, Caryl Bryer Fallert, Nancy Crow, Deidre Scherer, Michael Godfrey, and Priscilla Hair for the work they have done that inspires me.

MY KALEIDOSCOPE QUILT

On the last day of my first visit to Paducah, I visited MAQS and learned about this contest. I came away with a dream that some day I might have a quilt on exhibit there.

That night, while waiting for my dinner order, I began sketching on the placemat. That sketch was the initial drawing that became BUSBY BERKELEY'S BUTTERFLY BALLET. I am still amazed that the finished quilt looks so similar to that sketch.

The fabric is 100% cotton, except for tulle used for the chenille butterflies (the only design not mine; it is The Stencil Co.'s SCL-167-05). I prefer using silk-finish thread, though some monofilament was used to couch braid. I employed techniques that I had not tried before, like double threads in the needle for quilting, drafting stretched and expanded blocks, and couching chenille or braid. The fast-turn appliqué method was very useful for the petals and leaves in the center "courtyard."

One day, I was watching a biography of Busby Berkeley as I worked. He produced and choreographed many of the Esther Williams aquatic ballets, featuring kaleidoscopic movements. This gave me the name for the quilt.

I learned an enormous amount about quilting in challenging myself to find ways to bring that initial sketch into reality.

"Envisioning a quilt and bringing it to fruition has sometimes meant waiting until I have learned a new technique."

Finalist

Southwestern Eclipse
60" x 60", 1998
Cotton fabric
Machine pieced and quilted

Sue Turnquist

Harrisburg, Missouri

MY QUILTING

I will never know what possessed me to begin shopping for a sewing machine during the summer of 1995. I hadn't used a machine in nearly 20 years, and I was perplexed when the sales lady asked me what kind of sewing I wanted to do. I pondered the question for a few seconds and said, "I want to make quilts." I still don't know why the word "quilts" jumped into my head so readily, but it has since become a wonderful obsession.

I made my first quilt, a small Nine Patch with machine-embroidered leaves. I gleaned as much information from books and the Internet as I could before taking a basic machine-piecing class just to make sure I was on the right track.

I appreciate traditional quilts, but art quilts excite me. The works of Caryl Bryer Fallert, Ellen Anne Eddy, Jane Herbst, Charlotte Warr Andersen, and Susan Carlson send my heart racing. All of my piecing and quilting is done by machine. Free-motion quilting and free-motion embroidery are my passions.

I work as a veterinary pathologist, and I am fortunate to have a husband who understands why I need three sewing machines and more fabric than I can possibly use in my lifetime.

MY KALEIDOSCOPE QUILT

I am a procrastinator, and I am still amazed that SOUTHWESTERN ECLIPSE was finished in time to enter this contest. I designed the quilt on the computer, but shortly before the deadline, the computer died and I lost all of my designs. I moved on to graph paper and tried to reproduce the designs from memory.

I recruited fabrics that I had set out for another quilt. Batiks really catch my eye, and I had fallen in love with the lighter tan batik with the purple, blue-green, and midnight blue highlights. I had several commercial cotton blue-green and purple fabrics and was trying to decide which to use when I remembered some advice from a Doreen Speckman workshop: when dealing with colors of the same value, use several fabrics to add interest. I strip pieced the fabrics and then cut wedges with a kaleidoscope template.

I played with the cut wedges on the design wall until the design pleased me. Before I could start piecing, a pipe above my design wall began leaking, and I had to move the wedges to another wall.

I used Marti Michell's method for piecing Kaleidoscope blocks, and assembly was nearly trouble-free. I was working on the last border when I realized I had cut the strip too narrow and had used all of the fabric. Fortunately, it was still available at the fabric store.

"No other creative media I have experienced provides the same creative high."

BASIC BLOCK

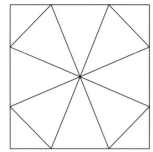

Included in this section are full-size templates for traditional Kaleidoscope blocks in four sizes. Select the size most appropriate for your fabrics and project plans. You will also find some Kaleidoscope quilt design ideas to jump-start your imagination.

See how many designs you can find in this traditional quilt. Please feel free to copy this page and try your own coloring ideas.

KALEIDOSCOPE QUILT DESIGNS, BASIC BLOCK

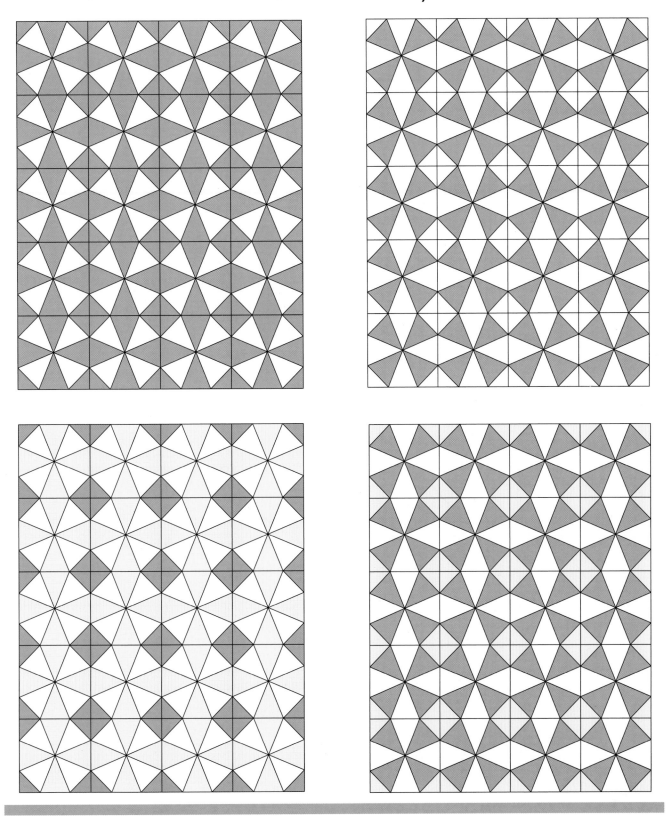

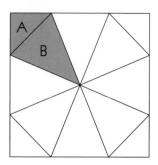

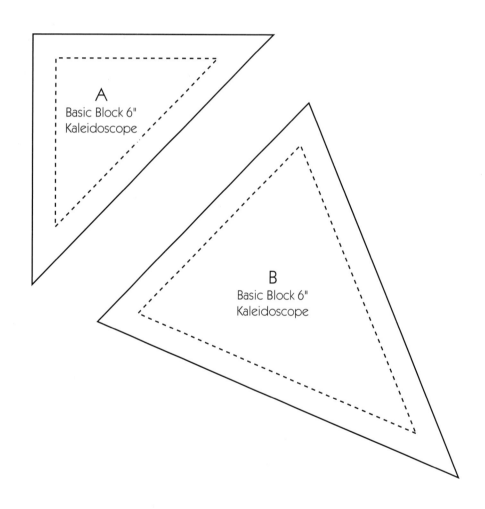

A
Basic Block 6"
Kaleidoscope

B
Basic Block 6"
Kaleidoscope

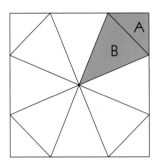

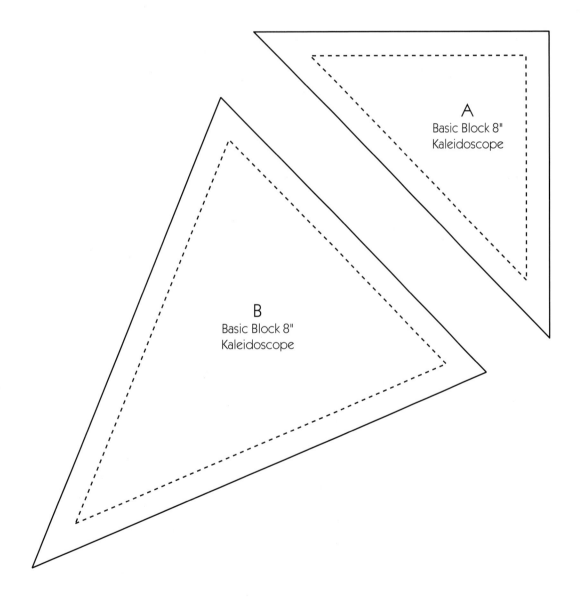

A
Basic Block 8"
Kaleidoscope

B
Basic Block 8"
Kaleidoscope

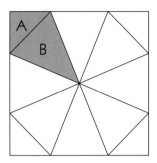

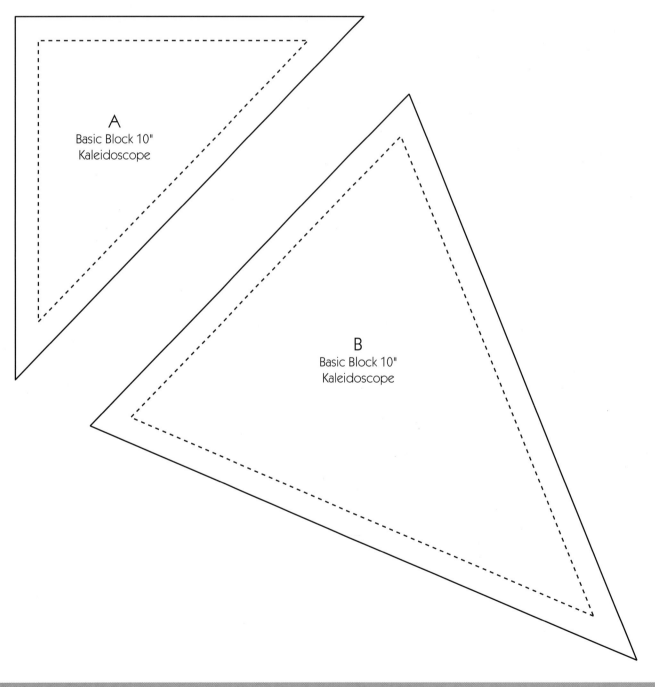

A
Basic Block 10"
Kaleidoscope

B
Basic Block 10"
Kaleidoscope

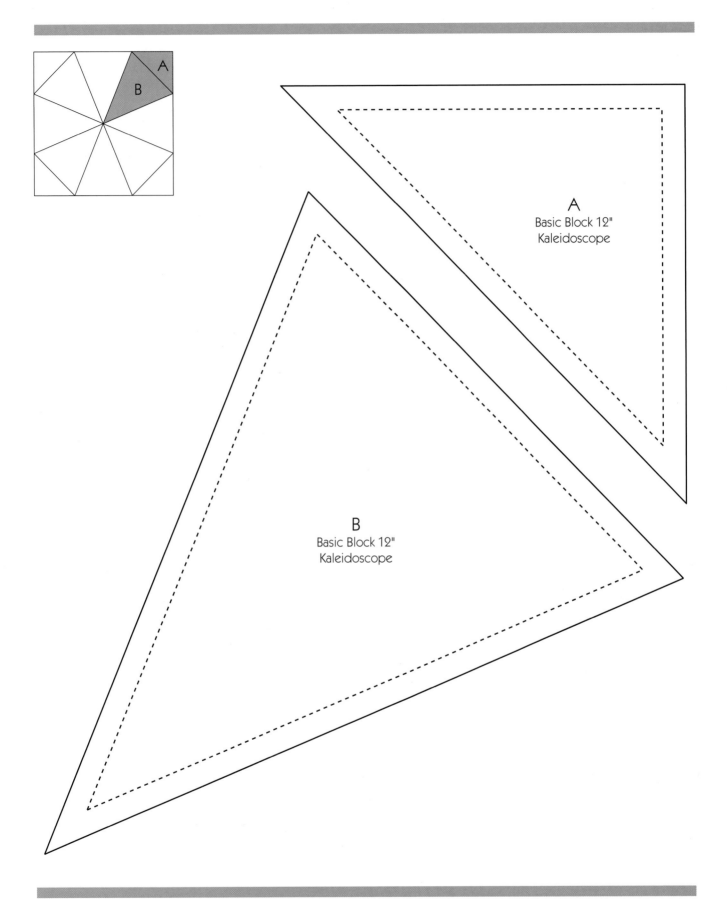

A
Basic Block 12"
Kaleidoscope

B
Basic Block 12"
Kaleidoscope

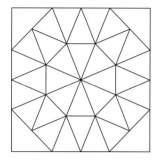

BLOCK VARIATION

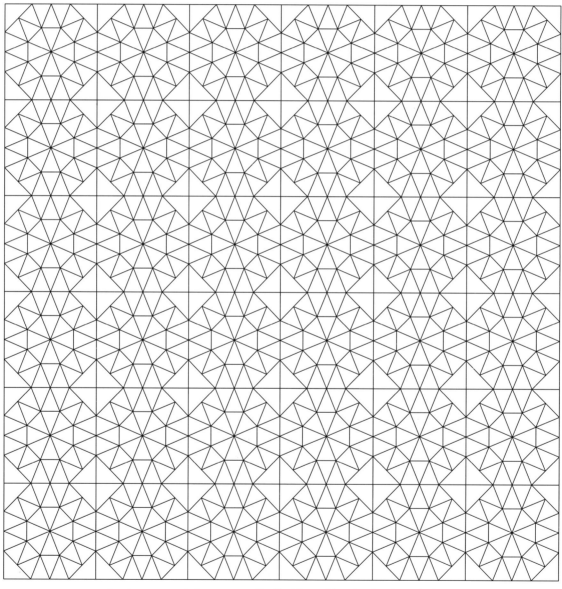

See how many designs you can find in this traditional quilt. Please feel free to copy this page and try your own coloring ideas.

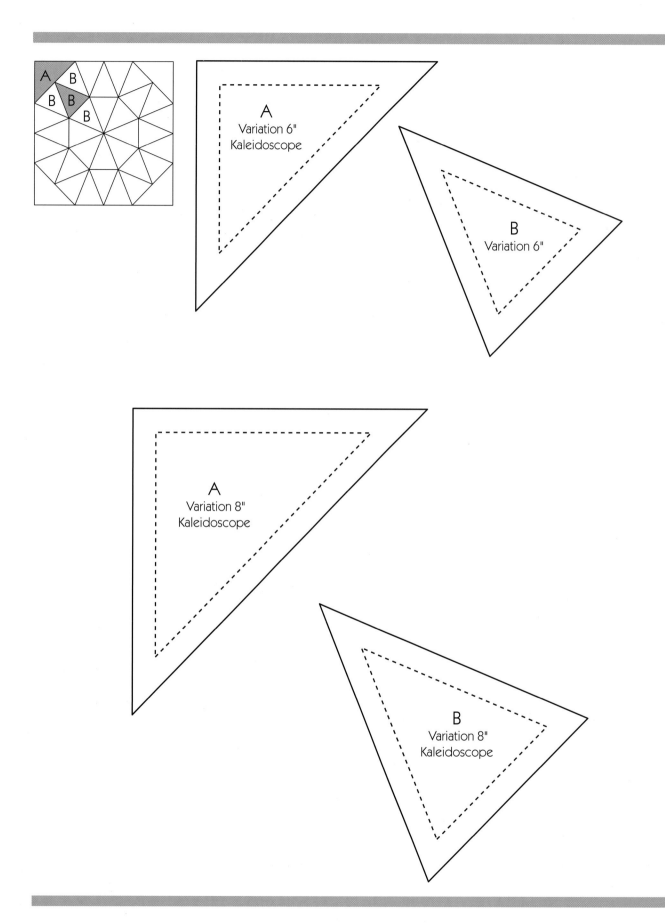

A
Variation 6"
Kaleidoscope

B
Variation 6"

A
Variation 8"
Kaleidoscope

B
Variation 8"
Kaleidoscope

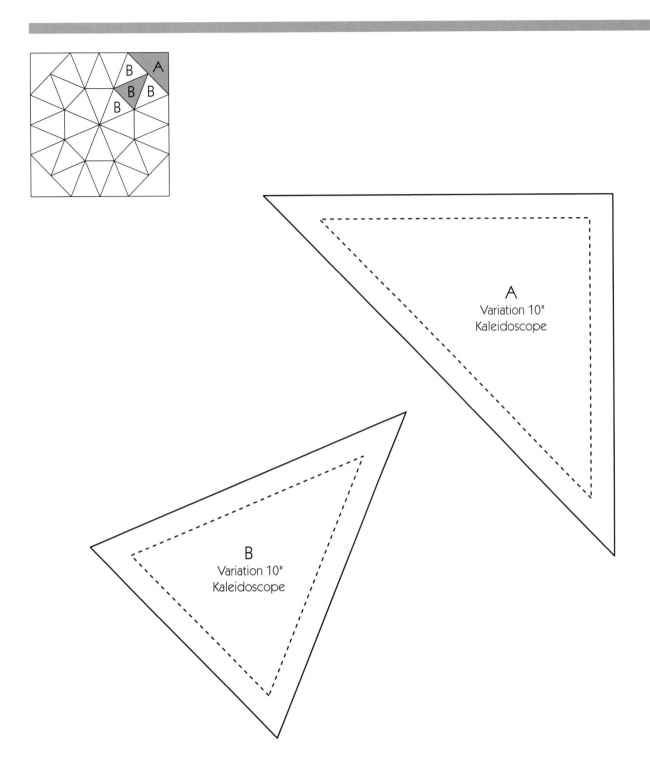

A
Variation 10"
Kaleidoscope

B
Variation 10"
Kaleidoscope

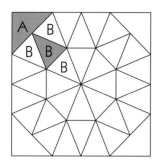

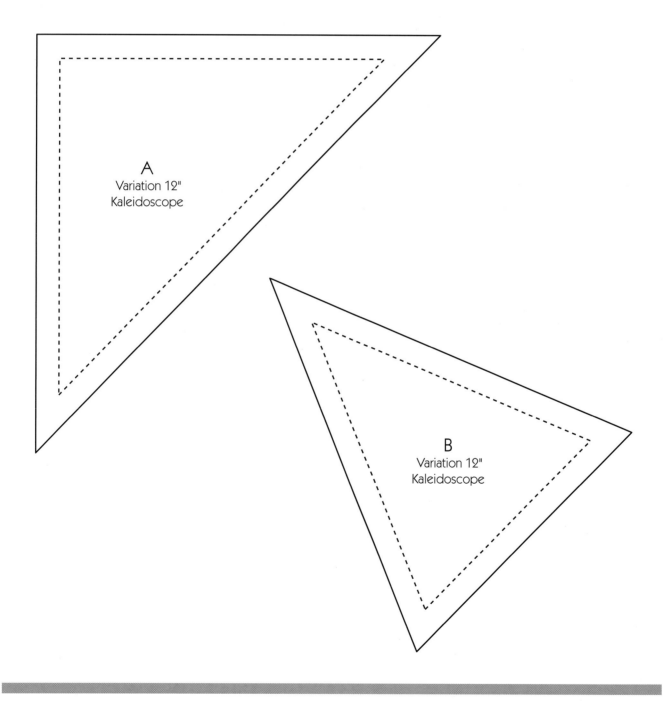

A
Variation 12"
Kaleidoscope

B
Variation 12"
Kaleidoscope

LIFE'S LITTLE SURPRISES, detail, 62" x 65", 1998, by Sherry Chan. Full quilt is shown on page 26.

MAKING WAVES
BY IZUMI TAKAMORI

GEM STONES is made from three distorted blocks to create a wave effect. The quilt is assembled in vertical rows. The two B rows are the same, but one is turned upside down. The four rows A, B, C, B (upside down), are repeated four times across the quilt to create this intriguing design. Foundation piecing patterns are provided.

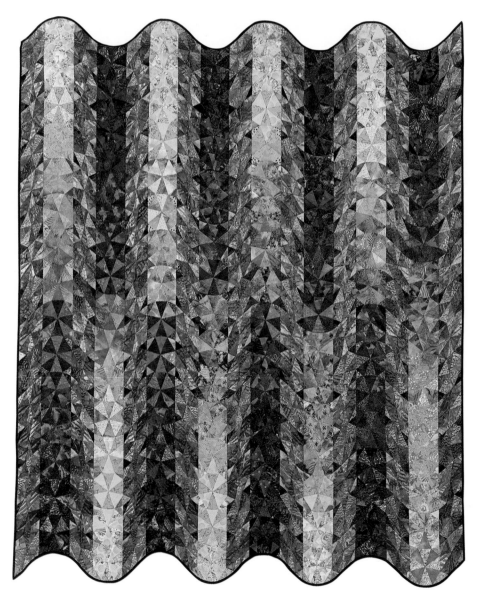

GEM STONES, 77½" x 92½", 1998, by Izumi Takamori.

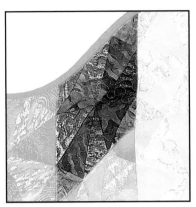

Block A

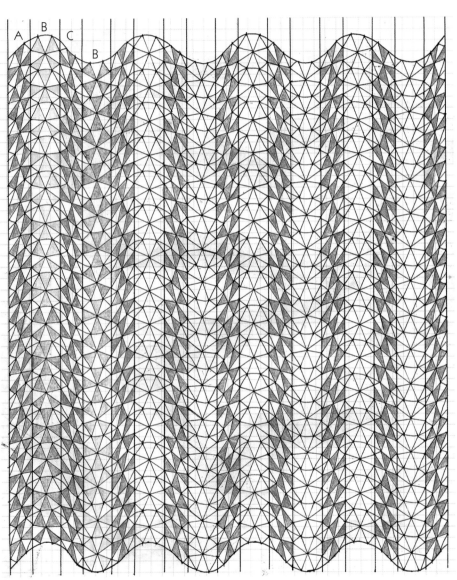

This is Izumi's original drawing of GEM STONES.

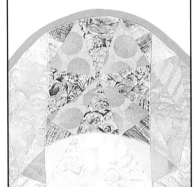

Block B

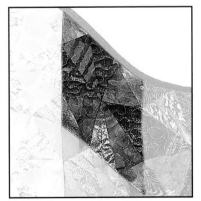

Block C

GEM STONES
FOUNDATION PIECING PATTERN
BLOCK A

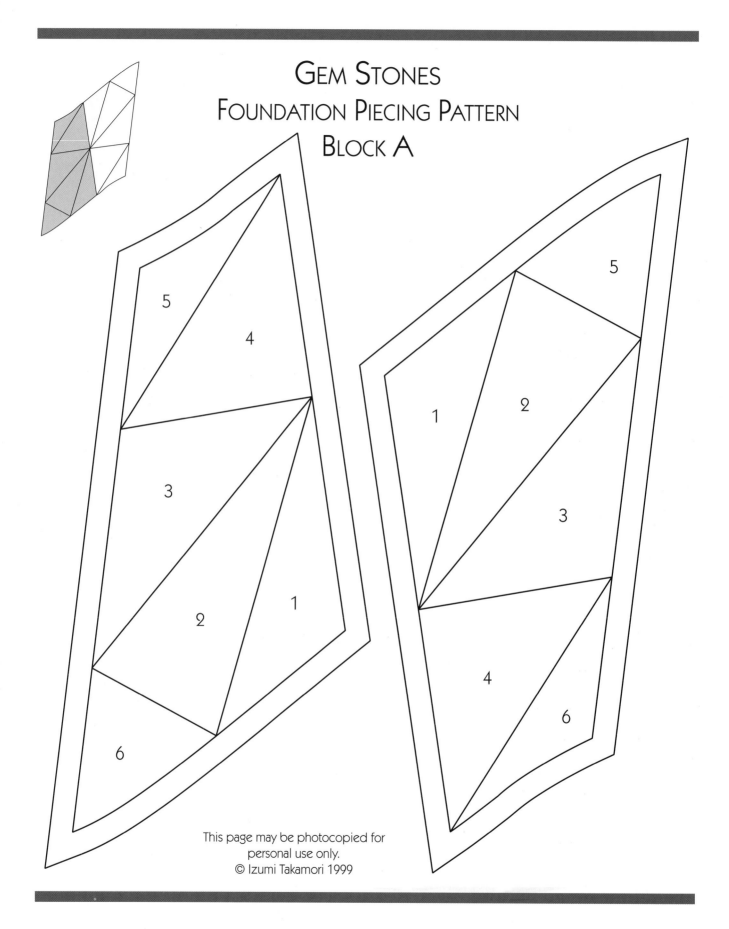

This page may be photocopied for
personal use only.
© Izumi Takamori 1999

This page may be photocopied for
personal use only.
© Izumi Takamori 1999

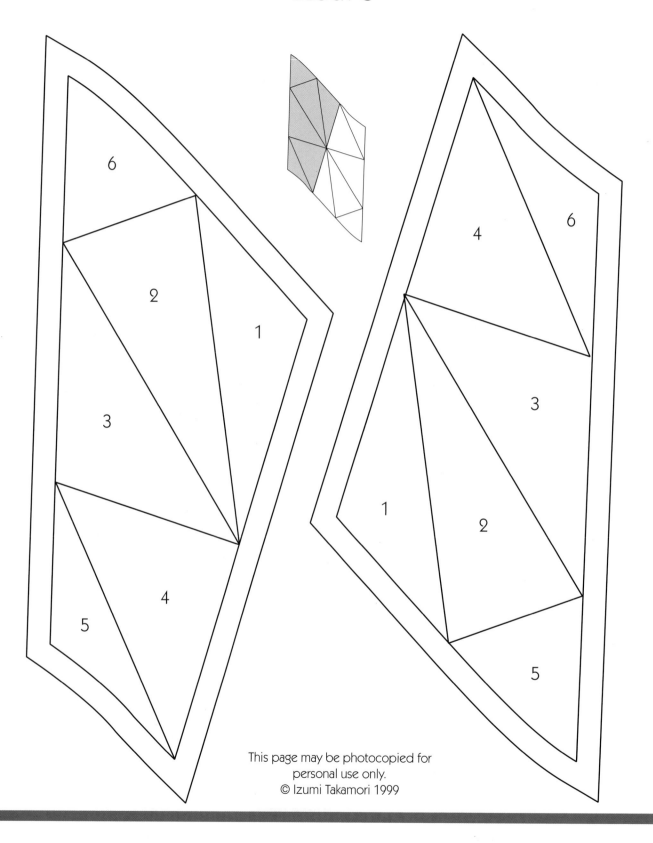

This page may be photocopied for
personal use only.
© Izumi Takamori 1999

FOUNDATION PIECING PATTERN
BY ANJA TOWNROW

Most of my quilts are planned on large sheets of paper. SPINNING WHEEL consists of one giant Kaleidoscope block with borders, so I drew one full-size wedge and one corner triangle. Then, I had fun drawing a design inside the wedge with a ruler and compasses. After rejecting the first design, I drew another and cut the second drawing into templates and sections for foundation piecing.

To make your own small Kaleidoscope quilt (approximately 23½" square), similar to SPINNING WHEEL, trace the wedge sections (pgs. 66-68), transferring all marks. You will need eight tracings of each one.

Foundation piece sections A, C, and D. Trim the sections ¼" away from the paper for seam allowances. Then, on the wrong side of the fabric, draw seam lines and matching marks around the paper foundations. Remove the paper.

Assemble the wedges, using the matching marks to help you align the pieces. Sew the wedges together to form the kaleidoscope shape and add the corner triangles (p. 69).

SPINNING WHEEL, 66" x 66", 1998, by Anja Townrow.

Anja's original drawings for the pattern presented on pages 66 and 67.

SPINNING WHEEL
FOUNDATION PIECING
PATTERNS

SECTION A

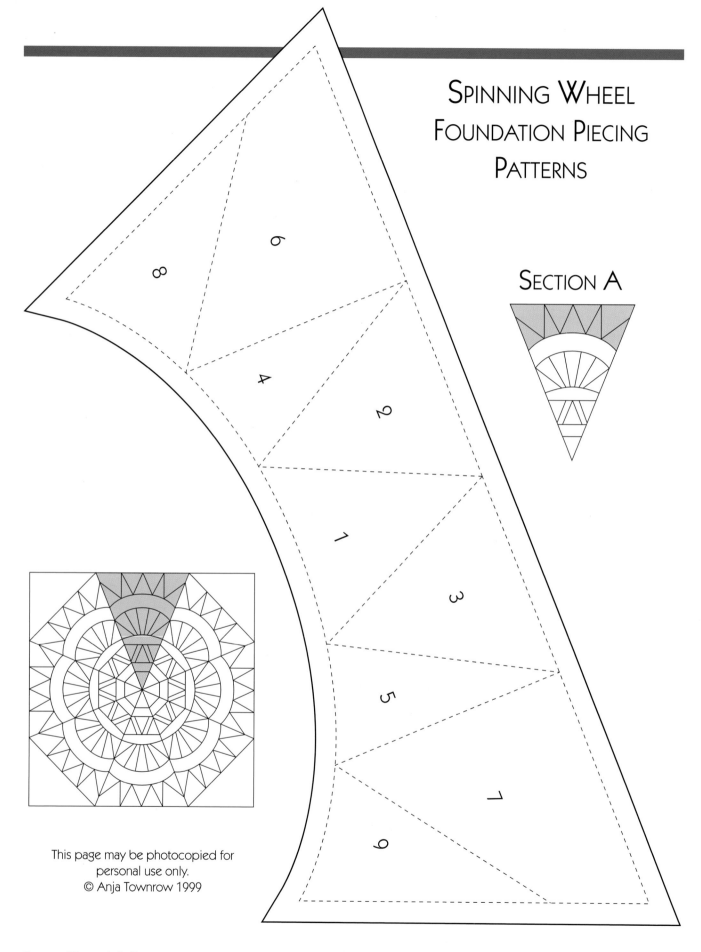

This page may be photocopied for
personal use only.
© Anja Townrow 1999

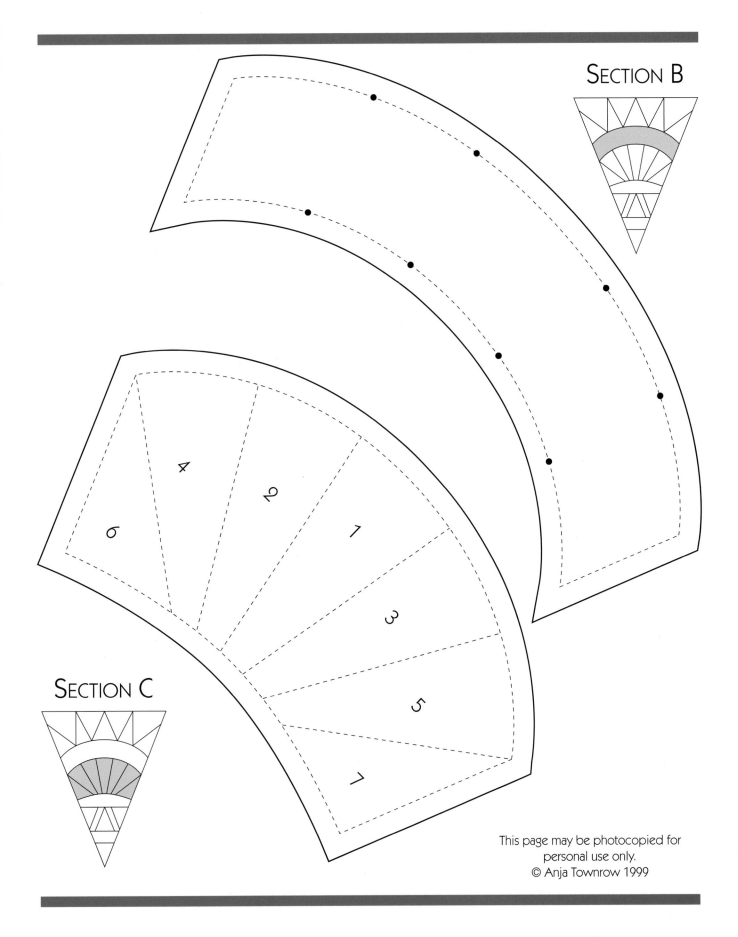

SECTION B

SECTION C

4

2

6

1

3

5

7

This page may be photocopied for
personal use only.
© Anja Townrow 1999

SPINNING WHEEL
FOUNDATION PIECING PATTERNS

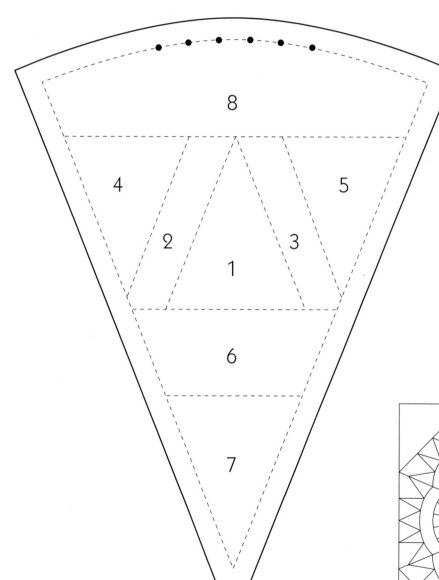

8

4

5

2

3

1

6

7

This page may be photocopied for
personal use only.
© Anja Townrow 1999

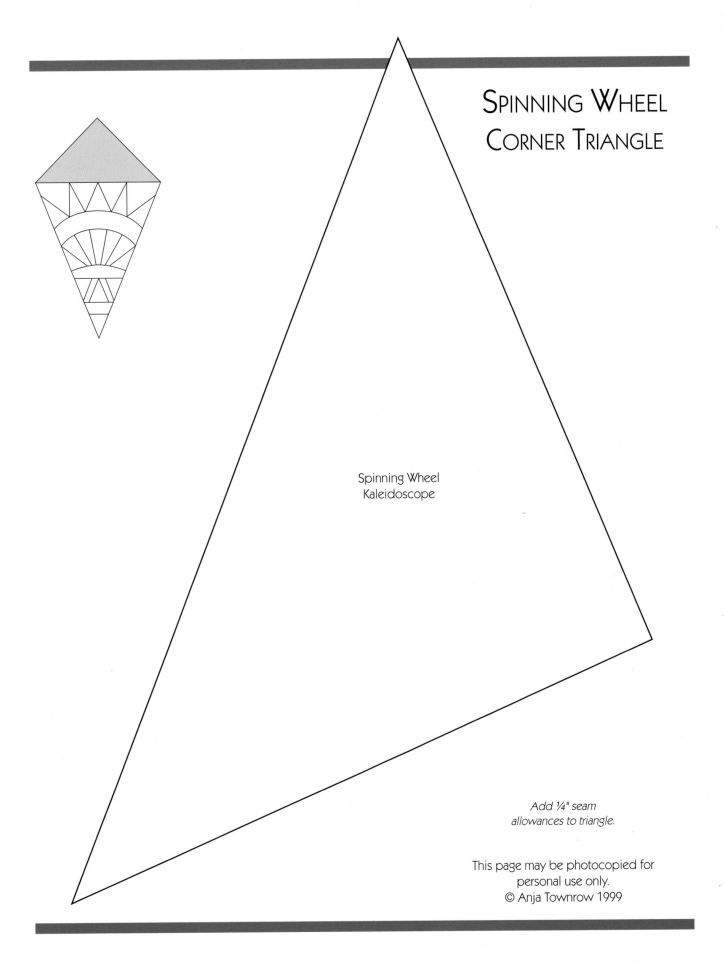

Spinning Wheel
Kaleidoscope

*Add ¼" seam
allowances to triangle.*

This page may be photocopied for
personal use only.
© Anja Townrow 1999

SECONDARY DESIGNS

BY LAURA A. PARK

The Kaleidoscope block is particularly fascinating because the repetition of motifs can carry the design across seam lines. If a carefully designed block is repeated in a standard side-by-side arrangement, it is possible for the finished quilt to appear to be made from three different blocks. Kaleidoscope 42, one of the blocks in SMOKE AND MIRRORS II, illustrates this idea. The block has a strong center, consisting of four large, green leaves, arranged in a four-leaf-clover fashion.

A secondary design, formed where the corners of four blocks meet, gives the appearance of a second block, which has as much or more prominence as the first one.

The third block appears where the sides of two adjacent blocks touch each other. In Kaleidoscope 42, the third block is a mirror-image leaf design. The change in color and the crispness of the leaf motif strengthen the illusion of another block.

Kaleidoscope 42.

Kaleidoscope 42 secondary design.

SMOKE AND MIRRORS II, 64" x 64", 1998, by Laura A. Park. This quilt is made from the Kaleidoscope 42 block alternated checkerboard style with a more flowery block.

Appliqué Animals
by Marta Amundson

My concern over environmental issues in Australia inspired the design for ALMOST PARADISE. The animal shapes I quilted represent all of the beautiful creatures threatened by habitat loss. The animal patterns on the next two pages can be used for appliqué, embroidery, or quilting.

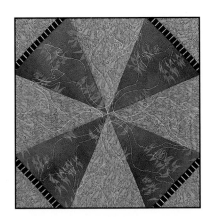

Kangaroos.

Crocodiles.

ALMOST PARADISE, 63" x 63", 1998, by Marta Amundson.

ANIMAL PATTERNS
Use these patterns for appliqué, embroidery, or quilting.

This page may be photocopied for
personal use only.
© Marta Amundson 1999

LET THE FABRIC BE YOUR GUIDE
BY ANN HARWELL

The techniques I used to create BALANCE THE SCALES OF WORLD JUSTICE are an amalgamation from four books written by Georgia Bonesteel, Jinny Beyer, Ruth McDowell, and Paula Nadelstern. Using a 45°-angle ruler centered on a piece of graph paper, I drew a triangle, adding length to the angle as I designed the quilt. I sketched an outline of the scales of justice at the wide end of the triangle to serve as a guide for fabric placement.

Using graph template material, I cut individual templates for each of the fabrics and I used a permanent pen to mark the template with the fabric design.

When I finished designing and piecing all eight triangles, I placed them on my design wall for consideration. At this point, I decided against squaring off the piece. It seemed to suit the theme of "balance" better as an octagon.

Finally, I put together all eight triangles to complete the octagonal top. To enhance the individual fabrics and help them convey their message of liberty, justice, and equality, I hand quilted around the fabric design lines. I took care to emphasize with my quilting the words and pictures that best describe the theme.

Detail from BALANCE THE SCALES OF WORLD JUSTICE, 62" x 62", 1998, by Ann Harwell.

PERSIAN FANTASY II PATTERN
BY ARLEEN BOYD

Inspiration for a quilt design can come from almost anywhere. The idea for PERSIAN FANTASY II, featured on page 24, was delivered right to my mailbox in the form of an advertisement for Oriental carpets. One carpet caught my eye and sparked my imagination, and so the idea for the quilt was born.

Combining the timeless beauty of an Oriental carpet with the modern practicality of a basic computer drawing program, I soon had a few ideas on paper. I simplified my first design, leaving out the wide sashing and the six small Kaleidoscope blocks on two sides of the center medallion. My center medallion design is based on an 18" Kaleidoscope wedge made of 26 pieces. After adding the corner triangles, the central square is 36" x 36".

In the simplified version you can see how I colored some wedges with colored pencils, then glued the wedges onto a separate sheet of paper to get the overall look of the design (p. 76). The decorative striped fabric in the border was one I had in my stash, but it had to be pieced in two places to make it long enough to fit. Can you find where it's pieced?

Quilting around the motifs and patterns in the fabric gave them the special emphasis I wanted. In the places where the fabric design had narrow parallel lines, I stitched along the lines to form narrow channels, then stuffed the channels with yarn to add more dimension.

Original version.

Simplified version.

PERSIAN FANTASY II, 57" x 68", 1996, by Arleen Boyd.

Original drawing of quilt design.

PERSIAN FANTASY II in progress. Detail of center medallion.

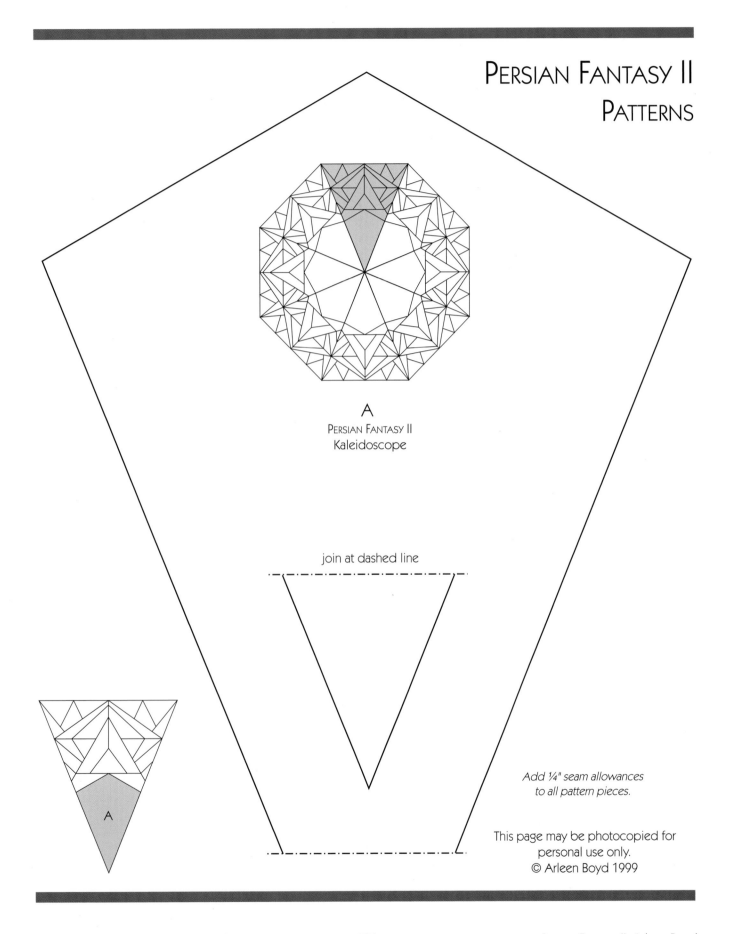

A
PERSIAN FANTASY II
Kaleidoscope

join at dashed line

*Add ¼" seam allowances
to all pattern pieces.*

A

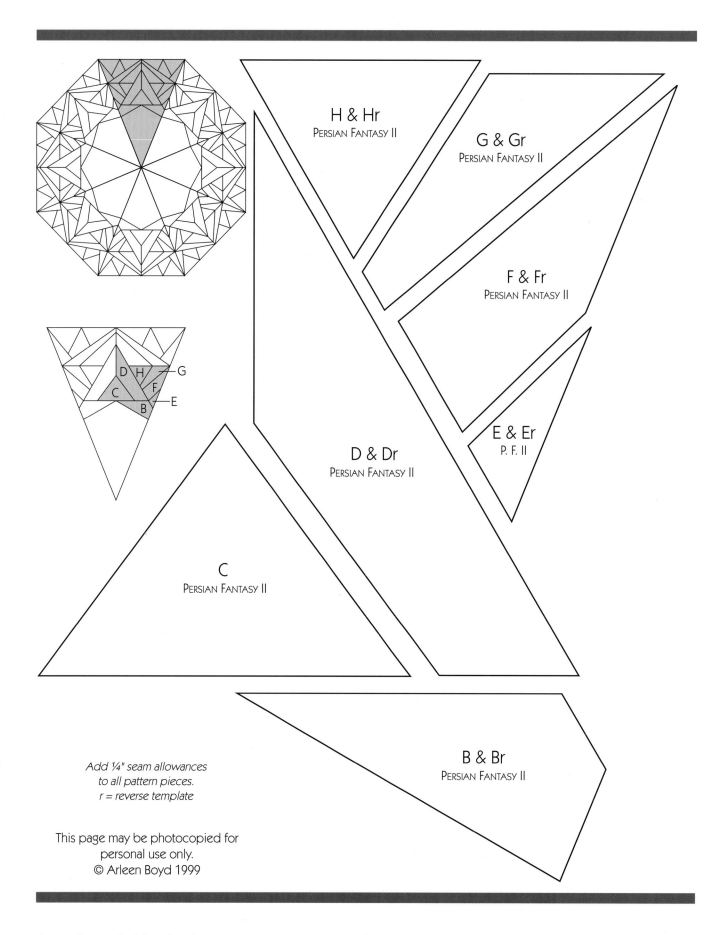

H & Hr
PERSIAN FANTASY II

G & Gr
PERSIAN FANTASY II

F & Fr
PERSIAN FANTASY II

D H G
C F
B E

D & Dr
PERSIAN FANTASY II

E & Er
P. F. II

C
PERSIAN FANTASY II

*Add ¼" seam allowances
to all pattern pieces.
r = reverse template*

B & Br
PERSIAN FANTASY II

This page may be photocopied for
personal use only.
© Arleen Boyd 1999

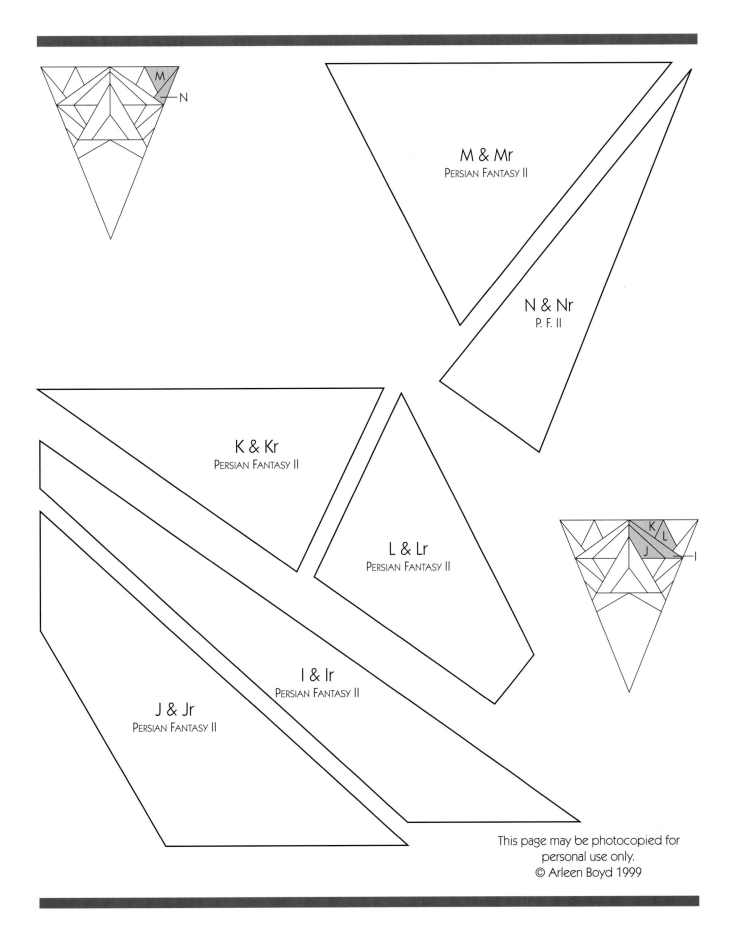

M & Mr
PERSIAN FANTASY II

N & Nr
P. F. II

K & Kr
PERSIAN FANTASY II

L & Lr
PERSIAN FANTASY II

I & Ir
PERSIAN FANTASY II

J & Jr
PERSIAN FANTASY II

KEEPING YOUR SANITY WHILE QUILTING
BY LAURIE SHEELEY

Throughout my years of quilting, I have made a few discoveries I would like to share with you. These bits of wisdom have helped me immensely, and I am hopeful you, too, will reap their benefits.

• When organizing fabric scraps for a scrap quilt, I sort by color and/or value and place the scraps in shoe boxes lined up along the back of my sewing table. I label each box according to color or value. The boxes are close enough that I can grab scraps of fabric without getting up from my machine. When the scraps are all sorted, it becomes easy to spot any that do not belong in that particular color or value category. Stir the scraps around in the boxes a couple of times and look for any offending scraps.

• Buy lots of shoes. The boxes are invaluable.

• I usually make at least one test block when I begin a project. There is nothing so rotten as cutting out an entire project only to find that an instruction or measurement was misread.

• Measure everything precisely, especially sashings, borders, and bindings. If you are not careful, you could make the perfect quilt only to find that the edges ruffle.

• Right in the middle of some projects, I start thinking they look stupid and ugly. I call this the adolescent stage of a quilt. Then I start thinking I am stupid and ugly, and on and on this thinking can go until creative paralysis sets in. This is a good time to do something positive: move forward rapidly to get past this phase or call someone who thinks you are smart and cute.

Cartoon by Michael Buckingham, 1999.

• Always clean your sewing room before starting a new project. I also put away any unfinished projects that might distract me or make me feel guilty. During the design and construction phases of a project, my sewing room looks as if a fabric bomb exploded, but I always start out tidy. It is good for the creative soul.

• I look at my project through the wrong end of a pair of binoculars to check for value, color placement, and continuity of design. Try it, you'll like it.

• Color is important, but I think value is even more important. A quilt can be made with exquisite colors and fabrics, but if the values are all the same, it will put the viewer to sleep.

• I sometimes have trouble convincing myself to try something new. That's when I turn to a quilting friend for help. Find one or more of these for yourself. They are as good as sisters.

• If you find someone who loves your quilts, love them back.

• I share everything I know, or anything I know how to do, with anyone who is interested. When I do, I get back more than I give. This sort of thing sets up something in the universal continuum smitzcranium or something. It must be some sort of law. Don't break it.

• Give old, unfinished projects away – same for fabric. Those things will just drag you down. Giving them away will make someone else happy, and it will free you to start something new and wonderful.

A THEME-BASED DESIGN
BY YOSHIKO KOBAYASHI

The design for EARLY SPRING WOOD evolved from small drawings, which I colored in with colored pencils. The blocks were pieced on paper-foundation patterns cut from tracing paper. Fabric placement was based on the colored drawings.

I found it necessary to create my own pieced fabrics to achieve the look I was striving for. With a rotary cutter, I cut many strips, which I pieced together, then I cut my block pieces from the strip-pieced fabric.

In keeping with the theme of an early spring in the woods, I modified a sketch of a leaf from my sketchbook for the quilting designs (p. 85). I filled in much of the open spaces with this design. To create the illusion of the wind's movement through the woods, I quilted a meandering, loopy line around the outside of the quilt.

Gradation-dyed sashiko thread was used for quilting in the middle portion of the quilt. White quilting thread in the dark navy border emphasizes the flowing quilting design.

EARLY SPRING WOOD, 59" x 59", 1998, by Yoshiko Kobayashi.

EARLY SPRING WOOD PATTERNS

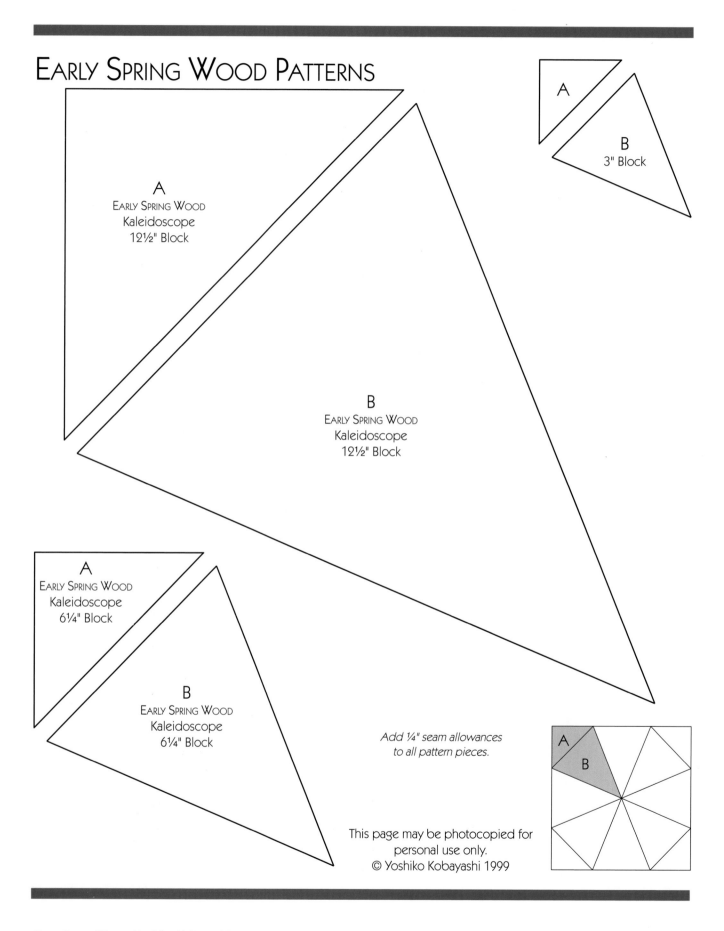

A

EARLY SPRING WOOD
Kaleidoscope
12½" Block

B

EARLY SPRING WOOD
Kaleidoscope
12½" Block

A

B
3" Block

A

EARLY SPRING WOOD
Kaleidoscope
6¼" Block

B

EARLY SPRING WOOD
Kaleidoscope
6¼" Block

*Add ¼" seam allowances
to all pattern pieces.*

A

B

This page may be photocopied for
personal use only.
© Yoshiko Kobayashi 1999

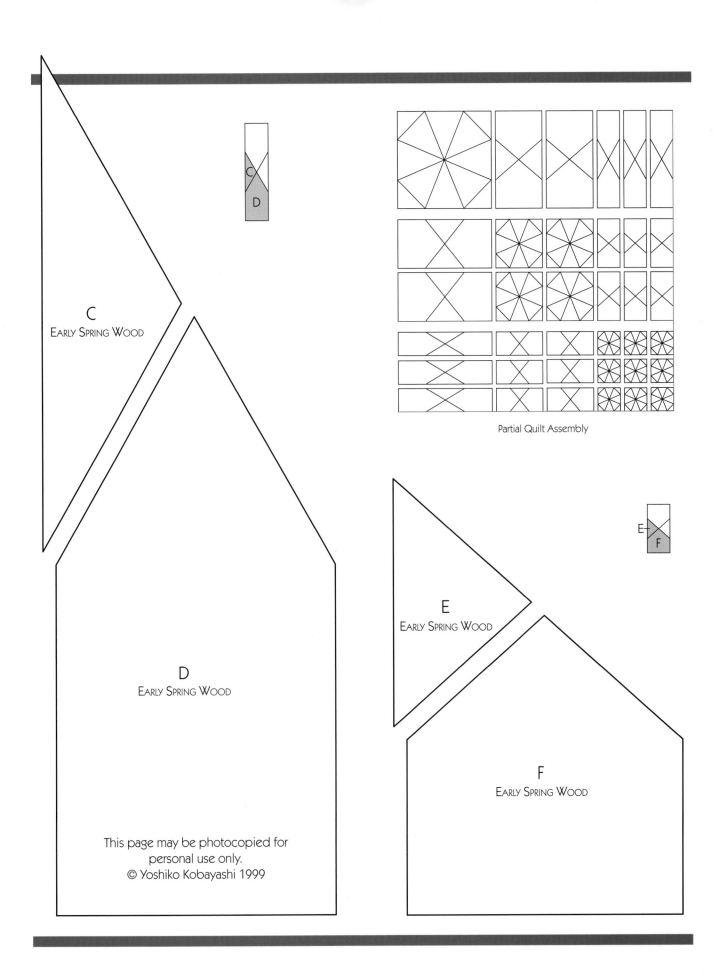

C

EARLY SPRING WOOD

D

EARLY SPRING WOOD

Partial Quilt Assembly

E

EARLY SPRING WOOD

F

EARLY SPRING WOOD

This page may be photocopied for
personal use only.
© Yoshiko Kobayashi 1999

EARLY SPRING WOOD PATTERNS

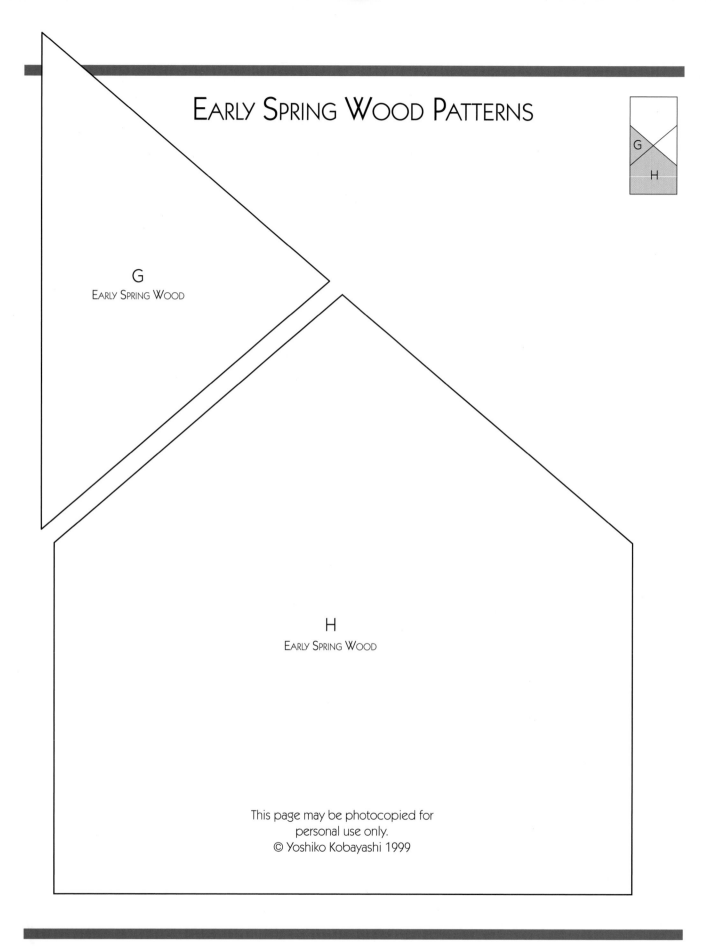

G
EARLY SPRING WOOD

H
EARLY SPRING WOOD

This page may be photocopied for
personal use only.
© Yoshiko Kobayashi 1999

Leaf Quilting Designs

DESIGNING WITH GRIDS
BY SUSAN MATHEWS

Over the years, I have worked with a number of traditional patterns that have the potential to form designs that give the illusion of curves in repeated blocks. The blocks that fall into this category include Storm at Sea, Pineapple, Judy in Arabia (designed by Jeffrey Gutcheon), and of course, the Kaleidoscope.

Generally, I photocopy the outline of many blocks and place them together on a page so that I have the basic grid that is peculiar to each pattern. I then let my eyes pick out different shapes that appear within the grid. The absence of the traditional block shading lets all sorts of possibilities emerge, and you will find many different shapes hidden in there.

A good way to use the grid is to overlay a piece of tracing paper on it and pay attention to the lines rather than the shapes. See what designs you can see in the grid.

I used to use colored pencils or a lead pencil to rough in these shapes that emerged from the grid. Now, I use a quilt program on the computer, which is much quicker. Sometimes, though, I resort to the old methods

MIDNIGHT FLOWERS, 60½" x 60½", 1994, by Susan Mathews.

because it is easier for me to work this way – a reflection of the fact that I was not born into the computer generation?

I never work all the details out on paper because I like to let the design evolve and take on a life of its own. Even if I spent the time to make a finished design on paper, I know I would change it in some way in response to working with the fabric.

Once I have the idea roughed out or have chosen a favorite design from a number of options, I move to my design wall. I work on a large piece of felt, which is ruled in a grid pattern to assist me in placing the patches. The grid also allows me the freedom to work where I want rather than in rows. Sometimes, I abandon the entire sketch after I start working on the design wall.

Computer generated designs, such as KALEIDO-SCOPE FLOWERS (top) and LILY POND (bottom) can be added to by using tracing paper overlays.

CRYSTAL VISION
BY LORI S. MOUM

The use of computer drawing and design programs makes it possible to see many design ideas in a short period of time. Although I did not use them exclusively, such programs were instrumental in my designing of CRYSTAL VISION.

Working with one quarter of the block, I tried several orientations before deciding on the one I liked best. On the bottom of page 89, you can see the difference between the block I chose and the same quarter-block with a different orientation.

Color placement can be determined with the use of a computer. If you do not have a color monitor and printer, you can work in black, white, and shades of gray to experiment with values.

CRYSTAL VISION, 74" x 74", 1998, by Lori S. Moum.

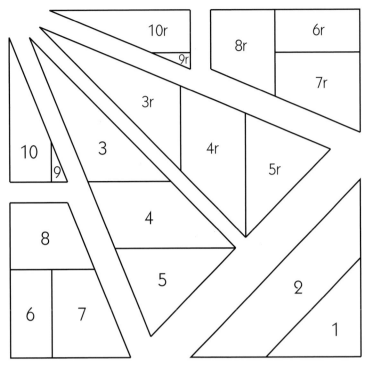

Quarter-block assembly. Pattern for 14" block on page 90.

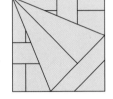

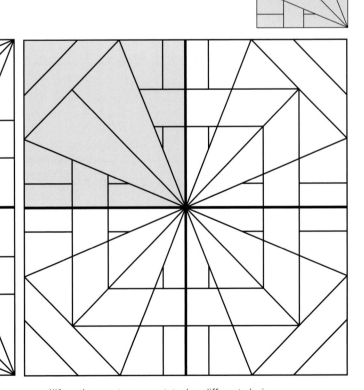

This is the block Lori chose for CRYSTAL VISION.

When the quarters are rotated, a different design emerges.

CRYSTAL VISION FOUNDATION PIECING PATTERN
14" BLOCK

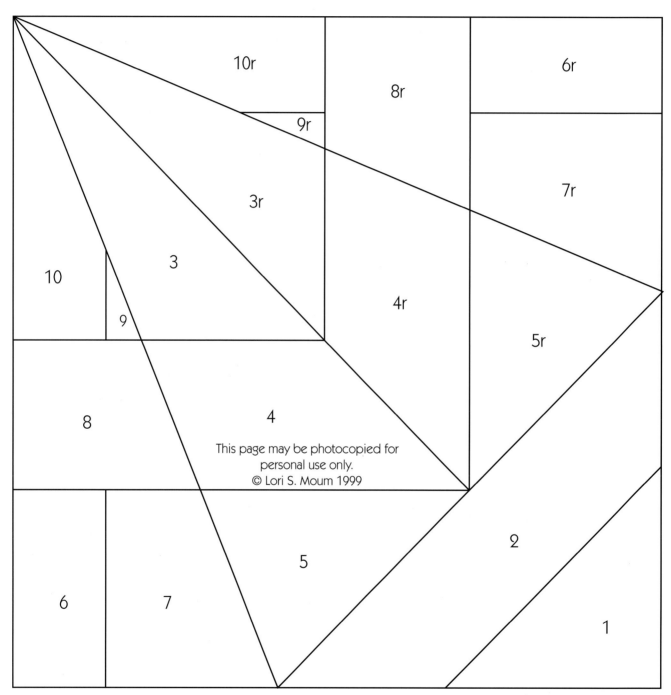

10r

8r

6r

9r

7r

3r

4r

3

5r

10

9

8

This page may be photocopied for
personal use only.
© Lori S. Moum 1999

4

2

5

6

7

1

Make a copy of this pattern for each quarter-block in your quilt. Paper piece the quarters in sections as shown in the Quarter-block assembly diagram on the preceding page. Add a ¼" seam allowance around the outside of the block.

HANGING AN ODD-SHAPED QUILT
BY JUDY SOGN

Because of its odd shape, hanging my quilt KALEI-DOSCOPES, DIAMONDS & STARS would be a problem, I realized. To provide the support the quilt needed, I placed a sleeve at the top of the widest part of the quilt. Then, to prevent the area above the sleeve from falling forward, I added two vertical casings, 1" wide, that run from the top of the quilt to the bottom of the sleeve (p. 92). These casings each hold a piece of stiff plastic that is the same length as the casing. Since they are stiff and they are located behind the sleeve and the hanging rod, they keep the quilt upright and against the wall.

KALEIDOSCOPES, DIAMONDS & STARS, 51" x 59", 1998, by Judy Sogn.

HANGING ODD SHAPES

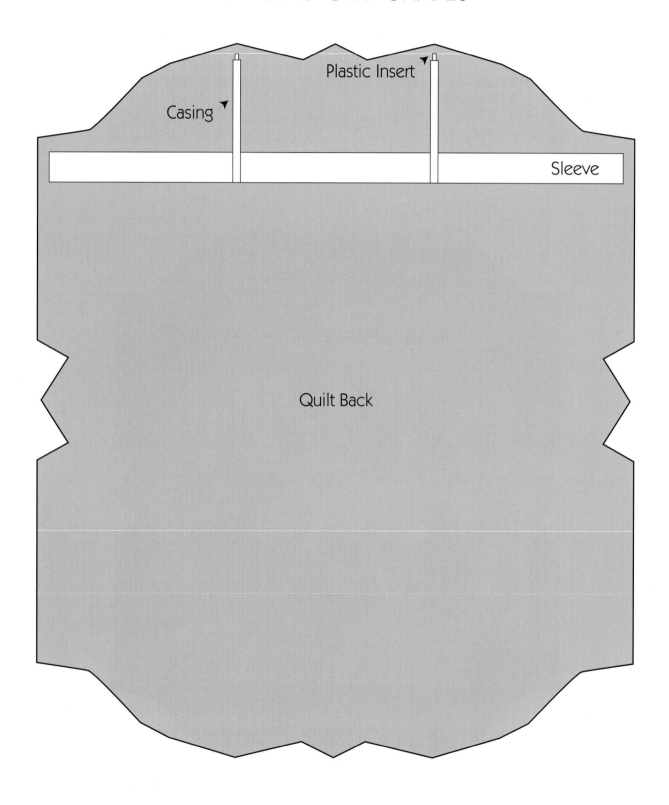

BUSBY BERKELEY'S BUTTERFLY PATTERN
BY BETH STEWART-OZARK

The butterflies that hold such prominent positions on BUSBY BERKELEY'S BUTTERFLY BALLET are cut from my own design. The appliquéd butterflies were first rough cut by rotary cutter, leaving at least a ¼" seam allowance all around. Each butterfly is made from four basic pieces. Within these pieces, each wing has 10 additional pieces. The center, or body, has two pieces (detail p. 94). The additional pieces are dictated by fabric choices. I used a combination of a fusible stabilizer and thread adhesive to stabilize the starched appliqué pieces before blind-hem stitching them to the larger butterfly shapes. Excess fabric was cut away underneath the piece.

I repeated the basic outline of the butterfly appliqué design in my continuous free-motion quilting design given on page 95. The pattern can be reduced or enlarged to suit your needs.

This design requires five runs around the quilt to complete it. I made a plastic template and then penciled the design on thin tracing paper for the top and bottom lines of the butterfly. The tracing paper was pinned to the border. First, I stitched line No.1. Line No. 2 was quilted next and the paper torn away. Line No. 3 was free-motion, eyeball-quilted, but it could easily be added to the tracing paper. Lines No. 4 and 5 were echo quilted ¼" from the butterfly.

BUSBY BERKELEY'S BUTTERFLY BALLET, 74" x 74", 1998, by Beth Stewart-Ozark.

BUTTERFLY APPLIQUÉ PATTERN

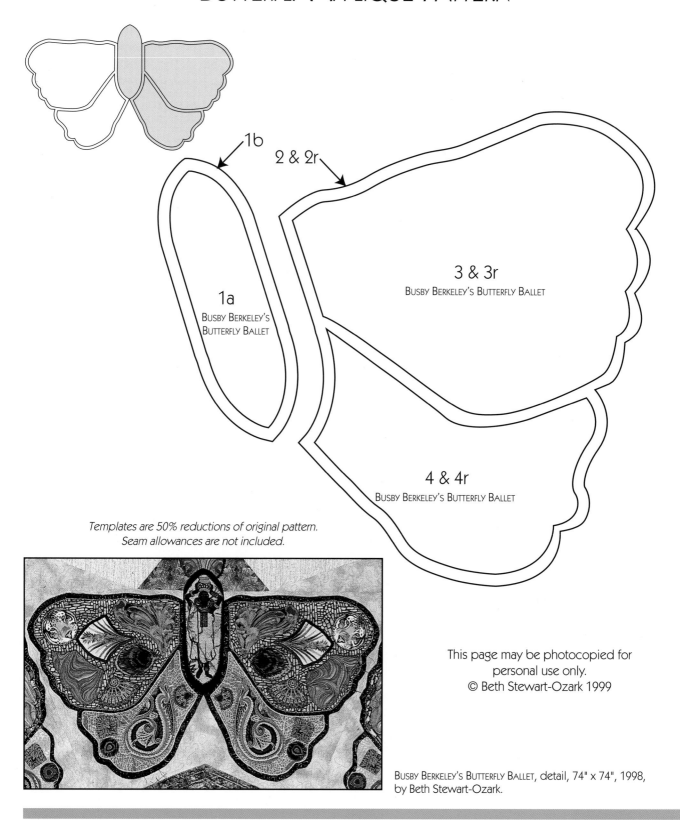

1b

2 & 2r

3 & 3r
BUSBY BERKELEY'S BUTTERFLY BALLET

1a
BUSBY BERKELEY'S
BUTTERFLY BALLET

4 & 4r
BUSBY BERKELEY'S BUTTERFLY BALLET

*Templates are 50% reductions of original pattern.
Seam allowances are not included.*

BUSBY BERKELEY'S BUTTERFLY BALLET, detail, 74" x 74", 1998,
by Beth Stewart-Ozark.

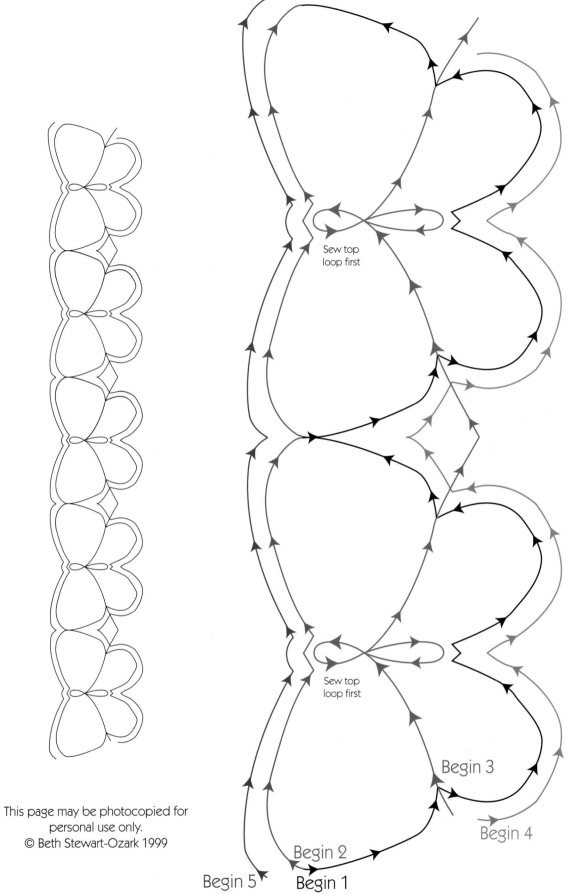

Sew top
loop first

Sew top
loop first

Begin 3

Begin 4

Begin 2

Begin 5   Begin 1

STRIP-PIECED KALEIDOSCOPE
BY VIRGINIA HOLLOWAY

The wedges in Virginia Holloway's Kaleidoscope quilt, called OPENING, are cut from strip-pieced bands. The narrow strips are cut ⅞" wide, and the wide strips 2". Sew the strips together as shown in the pattern, then make a template from the pattern or use a commercial 45° wedge ruler to cut the bands into wedges. (The seam lines can be marked on the template or ruler to aid in placement.) Blocks made from this pattern are 16" finished. This technique can be used to make wedges from strips of any width.

OPENING, 70" x 90", 1998, by Virginia Holloway.

OPENING WEDGE PATTERN

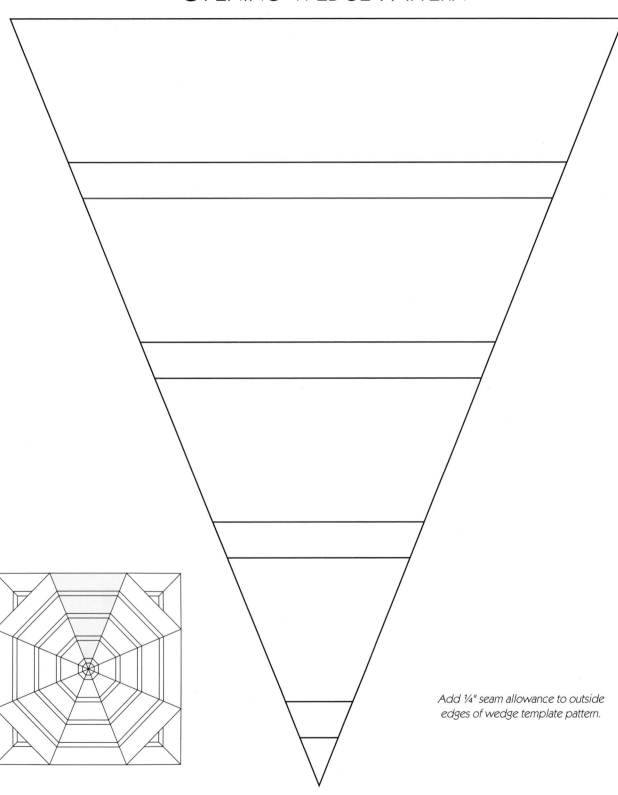

Add ¼" seam allowance to outside edges of wedge template pattern.

Opening Corner Triangle Pattern

The corner triangle can also be made from strip-pieced bands. Sew a ⅞" strip and a 2" strip together lengthwise. Cut into two pieces and join the two pieces end to end with a miter. Inset the small triangle in the miter (Y seam), then use a see-through template made from this corner triangle pattern to cut the corner piece to size.

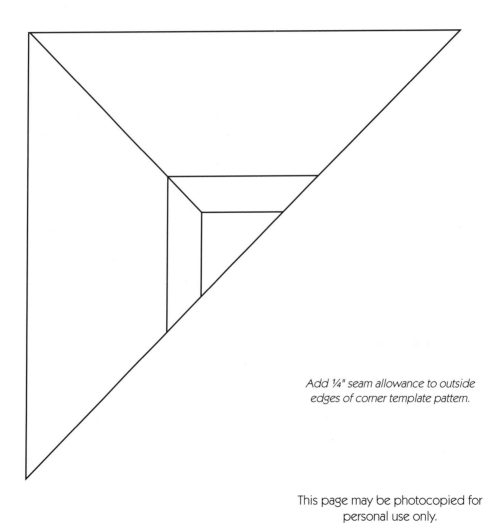

Add ¼" seam allowance to outside edges of corner template pattern.

FROM CONCEPT TO QUILT –
GETTING YOUR DESIGNS ON FABRIC
BY CLAUDIA CLARK MYERS

The techniques for putting the windmills on THE GATHERING STORM I learned from Caryl Bryer Fallert, Ruth McDowell, and Shirley Kirsch. From Caryl, I learned the design method of projection drawing and machine appliqué/piecing that I used to create the sky. Ruth McDowell's curved-seam piecing and Shirley Kirsch's hand-piecing and marking techniques proved invaluable in creating this piece. The tracing-paper embroidery technique is my own invention, I think.

After settling on the theme for my quilt, I began researching windmills. I found the three designs I wanted to use and did several small sketches of each one, refining them as I went. When I was satisfied with all three windmills, I transferred the sketches to plastic transparency sheets to be used with an overhead projector. I made one sheet for the background and one for each windmill.

With the projector, I enlarged the background sketch and redrew the lines on a piece of white paper pinned to the wall. I drew many matching marks across the seam lines. This paper became my background pattern for the quilt.

With the background still on the wall, I projected on it the drawings of the windmills. When I had each windmill positioned where I wanted and the size that I wanted, I marked its location on the background drawing with just a few lines to indicate where the bottom corners, the top, and the blades would be. I then placed another piece of paper on the background pattern in the appropriate area and drew

THE GATHERING STORM, 60" x 65", 1998, by Claudia Clark Myers.

the windmill onto it, creating a separate pattern. I pieced and appliqué/pieced the background, leaving space, plus seam allowances, for the windmills.

With more white paper, I traced over the windmill patterns and placed matching marks over the seam lines. I then cut the pieces apart and pieced each windmill. As I worked, I pinned each piece on the background to check the color. When the windmills were complete, I turned under a ¼" seam allowance on the outside edges, by using spray starch and an iron. The windmills were then machine appliquéd to the background with invisible thread and a tiny zig zag stitch.

Using the original windmill patterns, I added small details, such as windows and doors onto a fusible web, then ironed them in place and satin stitched around the edges.

The outlines of the windmill blades and the balconies were traced on tracing paper. I ironed stabilizer to the back of the quilt top in the areas where the blades and balconies would be, then pinned the tracing paper drawings to the front of the quilt. I straight stitched over all the lines to be embroidered, removed the tracing paper, then satin stitched one or two lines over the straight stitching. I removed the stabilizer only after I was happy with the way the seam looked.

Hint: Don't try to save time by zig-zagging over the tracing paper. You will have thousands of tiny paper flakes that even tweezers will not remove.

THE QUILTS

MUSEUM OF THE AMERICAN QUILTER'S SOCIETY
215 Jefferson Street, Paducah, Kentucky

A dream long held by American Quilter's Society founders Bill and Meredith Schroeder and by quilters worldwide was realized on April 25, 1991, when the Museum of the American Quilter's Society (MAQS, pronounced "Max") opened its doors in Paducah, Kentucky. As is stated in brass lettering over the building's entrance, this national non-profit institution is dedicated to "honoring today's quilter" by stimulating and supporting the study, appreciation, and development of quiltmaking throughout the world.

The 27,000 square foot facility includes a center exhibition gallery featuring a selection of the 184 quilts by today's quiltmakers comprising the Schroeder/MAQS Collection, and two additional galleries displaying exhibits of antique and other contemporary quilts. Lectures, workshops, and other related activities are also held on site, in spacious modern classrooms. A gift and book shop makes available a wide selection of fine crafts and over 400 quilt and textile books. The museum is open year-round, Monday through Saturday, and is wheelchair accessible.

For more information, write, MAQS, P.O. Box 1540, Paducah, KY 42002-1540, phone: 502-442-8856, or email: maqsmus@apex.net.

OTHER MAQS EXHIBIT PUBLICATIONS

OHIO STAR QUILTS
edited by Victoria Faoro
#4627: AQS, 1995, 112 pages, 8½" x 11", softbound, $16.95

PINEAPPLE QUILTS
edited by Barbara Smith
#5098: AQS, 1998, 104 pages, 8½" x 11", softbound, $16.95

MARINER'S COMPASS QUILTS
edited by Victoria Faoro
#4911: AQS, 1997, 112 pages, 8½" x 11", softbound, $16.95

20TH CENTURY QUILTS
by Cuesta Benberry and Joyce Gross
#4972: AQS, 1997, 32 pages, 5½" x 8½", softbound, $9.95

MINIATURE QUILTS: CONNECTING NEW AND OLD WORLDS
by Tina M. Gravatt
#4752: AQS, 1996, 64 pages, 8½" x 11", softbound, $14.95

FOUR BLOCKS CONTINUED...
by Linda Giesler Carlson
#4900: AQS, 1997, 128 pages, 8½" x 11", softbound, $16.95

These books can be found in the MAQS book shop and in local bookstores and quilt shops. If you are unable to locate a title in your area, you can order by mail from:

American Quilter's Society
P.O. Box 3290, Paducah, KY 42002-3290

Please add $1 for the first book and $.40 for each additional one to cover postage and handling. For international orders, please add $1.50 for the first book and $1 for each additional one.

To order by VISA or MASTERCARD, call toll-free:
1-800-626-5420 or fax: 1-502-898-8890

AQS BOOKS ON QUILTS

This is only a partial listing of the books available from the American Quilter's Society. AQS books are known worldwide for timely topics, clear writing, beautiful color photos, and accurate illustrations and patterns. The following books are available from your local bookseller, quilt shop, or public library. If you are unable to locate certain titles in your area, you may order by mail from the AMERICAN QUILTER'S SOCIETY, P.O. Box 3290, Paducah, KY 42002-3290. Add $2.00 for postage for the first book ordered and 40¢ for each additional book. Include item number, title, and price when ordering. Allow 14 to 21 days for delivery. Customers with Visa, MasterCard, or Discover may phone in orders from 7:00–5:00 CST, Mon.–Fri., 1-800-626-5420.